T0399628

Inquiry-Based Literature Instruction in the 6–12 Classroom

This practical and engaging book will help you learn how to teach literature with an inquiry-based approach. Inquiry-based literature instruction is an effective method to facilitate student engagement, motivation, and understanding in middle and high school English Language Arts (ELA) classrooms. Easy-to-implement and adaptable for many types of texts, this method encourages students to make authentic connections between texts, their lives, and real-world issues. In this classroom-ready resource, Ruday and Caprino walk through this instructional approach to demonstrate how using essential questions and a variety of texts will engage students in thought-provoking inquiry and promote meaningful learning.

This book features:

- Three inquiry-based units applicable for middle and high school ELA and English classrooms.
- A range of models of what inquiry-based literature instruction looks like in practice.
- A chapter on culturally responsive teaching and supporting English Language Learners (ELLs).
- Guides, templates, and resource lists to help you plan your own inquiry-based literature teaching.

Throughout the book Ruday and Caprino share a wealth of insights and resources to support you when putting inquiry-based instruction into practice.

Sean Ruday is Associate Professor of English Education at Longwood University, USA.

Katie Caprino is Assistant Professor of Education at Elizabethtown College, USA.

Other Eye on Education Books

Available from Routledge
(www.routledge.com/eyeoneducation)

The Multimedia Writing Toolkit:
Helping Students Incorporate Graphics and Videos
for Authentic Purposes, Grades 3–8
Sean Ruday

The Informational Writing Toolkit:
Using Mentor Texts in Grades 3–5
Sean Ruday

The Argument Writing Toolkit:
Using Mentor Texts in Grades 6–8
Sean Ruday

The Narrative Writing Toolkit:
Using Mentor Texts in Grades 3–8
Sean Ruday

The Elementary School Grammar Toolkit, Second Edition:
Using Mentor Texts to Teach Standards-Based Language and
Grammar in Grades 3–5
Sean Ruday

The Middle School Grammar Toolkit, Second Edition:
Using Mentor Texts to Teach Standards-Based Language
and Grammar in Grades 6–8
Sean Ruday

The Common Core Grammar Toolkit
Using Mentor Texts to Teach the Language Standards
in Grades 9–12
Sean Ruday

The First-Year English Teacher's Guidebook
Strategies for Success
Sean Ruday

Culturally Relevant Teaching in the English Language Arts Classroom
Sean Ruday

Matching Reading Data to Interventions
A Simple Tool for Elementary Educators
Jill Dunlap Brown and Jana Schmidt

Content Area Literacy Strategies that Work
Do This, Not That!
Lori G. Wilfong

Inquiry-Based Literature Instruction in the 6–12 Classroom

A Hands-on Guide for Deeper Learning

Sean Ruday and Katie Caprino

Routledge
Taylor & Francis Group

NEW YORK AND LONDON

First published 2021
by Routledge
52 Vanderbilt Avenue, New York, NY 10017

and by Routledge
2 Park Square, Milton Park, Abingdon, Oxon, OX14 4RN

Routledge is an imprint of the Taylor & Francis Group, an informa business

© 2021 Sean Ruday and Katie Caprino

Library of Congress Cataloging-in-Publication Data
Names: Ruday, Sean, author. | Caprino, Katie, author.
Title: Inquiry-based literature instruction in the 6–12 classroom : a hands-on guide for deeper learning / Sean Ruday and Katie Caprino.
Description: New York, NY : Routledge, 2021. | Includes bibliographical references.
Identifiers: LCCN 2020034477 (print) | LCCN 2020034478 (ebook) | ISBN 9780367569372 (hardback) | ISBN 9780367569358 (paperback) | ISBN 9781003099987 (ebook)
Subjects: LCSH: Inquiry-based learning. | Language arts (Middle school) | Language arts (Secondary) | English language—Study and teaching (Middle school)—Foreign speakers. | English language—Study and teaching (Secondary)—Foreign speakers.
Classification: LCC LB1027.23 .R83 2021 (print) | LCC LB1027.23 (ebook) | DDC 371.3—dc23
LC record available at https://lccn.loc.gov/2020034477
LC ebook record available at https://lccn.loc.gov/2020034478

ISBN: 978-0-367-56937-2 (hbk)
ISBN: 978-0-367-56935-8 (pbk)
ISBN: 978-1-003-09998-7 (ebk)

Typeset in Palatino
by Apex CoVantage, LLC

Access the Support Material: www.routledge.com/9780367569358

Contents

Meet the Authors

Sean Ruday is Associate Professor and Program Coordinator of English Education at Longwood University and a former classroom teacher. He began his teaching career at a public school in Brooklyn, New York, and has taught English and language arts at public and private schools in New York, Massachusetts, and Virginia. He holds a BA from Boston College, an MA from New York University, and a PhD from the University of Virginia. Some publications in which his works have appeared are *Issues in Teacher Education, Journal of Teaching Writing, Journal of Language and Literacy Education,* and *Contemporary Issues in Technology and Teacher Education.* This is Sean's twelfth book with Routledge Eye on Education. He frequently writes and presents on innovative ways to improve students' literacy learning. You can follow Sean on Twitter @SeanRuday and visit his website at www.seanruday. weebly.com.

Katie Caprino is Assistant Professor of PK-12 New Literacies at Elizabethtown College. She has taught middle and high school English at public schools in Virginia and North Carolina. She holds a BA in English from the University of Virginia, an MA in Education from the College of William and Mary, an MA in English from Old Dominion University, and a PhD from the University of North Carolina at Chapel Hill. Her articles have appeared in *Writing and Pedagogy, PA Reads, The ALAN Review, The History Teacher,* and *Teaching in Higher Education.* Katie is a frequent presenter at state and national conferences and enjoys presenting with undergraduate students. Her professional passions are children's, middle grades, and young adult literature; the teaching of writing; and technology integration in the literacy classroom. You can follow her on Twitter @KCapLiteracy.

Acknowledgments

Sean's Acknowledgments

I would like to thank the wonderful teachers, enthusiastic administrators, and supportive parents who welcomed me into their students' educational experiences and made it possible for me to teach the units described in this book. I had an amazing time working with their phenomenal students.

I would also like to thank the students who participated in the units described in this book, especially those who shared their reflections on their learning experiences. I am grateful to have worked with these talented and dedicated individuals.

I want to thank everyone at Routledge Eye on Education—especially phenomenal editor Karen Adler—for the insight, guidance, and support that makes this organization so exemplary.

I am grateful for David Magill, my department chair at Longwood University, for his continued support of my work and the leadership he provides.

I would like to thank my parents, Bob and Joyce Ruday. I am grateful for their encouragement in all aspects of my life.

Finally, I want to thank my wife, Clare Ruday. I can't imagine my life without the happiness she brings to it.

Katie's Acknowledgments

I want to first thank Sean for including me on this project and giving me this great opportunity. It's hard to believe that a chance social media meeting could have led to years of work on a book!

I returned to graduate school because I wanted to help teachers, and I am so grateful for those secondary literacy teachers who are guiding their students through inquiry on a daily basis.

I want to offer my appreciation for the editorial team at Routledge, most especially Karen Adler, who has championed this project from the day we met.

I want to thank my parents for their support of my teaching from the days when I tried to teach my little brother all that I knew. And, of course, thank you to Mike, who supported me throughout the writing of this book, and to my little boy, who has probably taught me the most about the true importance of inquiry in our world!

Support Material

The tools in the appendix can be downloaded, printed, and copied for classroom use. You can access these downloads by visiting the book product page on our website: www.routledge.com/9780367569358. Then click on the tab that says "Support Material" and select the files. They will begin downloading to your computer.

Section One
Key Background and Context

Introduction

What Is Inquiry-Based Literature Instruction?

If you looked into the classroom where Sean recently worked with an eighth-grade English class, you'd see an environment humming with the energy that comes from engaged, motivated students. If you stepped into the room, you'd hear students discussing wide-ranging texts that align with the essential questions they were studying. For example, you'd hear one student talking about how the messages of gender roles, struggle, and empowerment in Lizzo's music reflect themes she identified in Aisha Saeed's novel *Amal Unbound* and an article about the United States Women's National Soccer Team, explaining that all of these texts connect to the essential question she investigated: "Why is it important to challenge gender roles?"

Similarly, you'd hear another student discussing the essential question "What are the challenges we face when talking about mental health?" and making connections to the television show *This Is Us*, the novel *It's Kind of a Funny Story* by Ned Vizzini, and the poem "The Rider" by Naomi Shihab Nye. One visitor to the classroom asked these eighth-graders what they had been doing in English class recently. "We're talking about inquiry," one answered. "It's not like what we've done [in English class] before. Usually we read one book and take a test or write a paper. When we talk about inquiry, we think about a question. Then we read books and look at other texts, like poems, songs, and art, that help us answer that question."

Now, let's take a look at a different situation that further contextualizes possible practices of literature instruction. Sean recently had a conversation with a group of early-career English teachers about their classroom experiences. The discussion turned to the idea of instructional units: all of the teachers discussed units they taught on specific books—one taught a unit on *The Great Gatsby*, another on *To Kill a Mockingbird*, and another on *The Giver*. After the conversation, Sean reflected on what it might say about English instruction that so many of these units focused on single texts. "That's how I experienced English instruction as a student," he said to himself. "We would read a book, discuss it, and be assessed on it in some way. Reflecting on this approach, I can see issues with it. While I love sharing and discussing great works of literature with students, there are other ways to approach unit design and planning that allow for more wide-ranging, inclusive, and inquiry-oriented approaches to teaching literature."

Key Features of Inquiry-Based Literature Instruction

In the inquiry-oriented approach we describe in this book, students examine a work of literature and other related texts through the lens of one or more essential questions that require them to reflect on thought-provoking and relevant issues in the texts they consider (McTighe & Wiggins, 2013). These essential questions function as the basis for students' analyses and insights, which they continue to develop as the unit continues. As we discuss in this book, there are a variety of ways to incorporate inquiry-based literature instruction in the classroom. For example, in one model, students can read a whole-class book that the teacher combines with other texts, such as songs, poems, artwork, and short stories, that all address the essential question or questions. Another form involves more student choice in the inquiry-focused text the students use: in this model, the teacher identifies an essential question and asks the students to select texts they will read independently that relate to this question. A third model is even more student-driven: this version, which incorporates the features of Genius Hour—a time for students to pursue their own inquiry-based passion projects (Krebs & Zvi, 2015)—by asking students to come up with their own areas of inquiry and create their own lists of texts that align with their inquiry focus and corresponding essential questions. Examples of these three forms of inquiry-based English instruction are discussed in detail in this book.

While the specifics of particular units can vary, we present three belief statements that we feel can be used to maximize the effectiveness of all inquiry-based literature instruction:

◆ **Inquiry-based literature instruction is especially effective when it incorporates well-crafted essential questions.** Essential questions, which establish the framework for students' inquiry, are key aspects of this instructional approach. These questions guide students' analyses while also helping them think about texts in innovative ways. In this book, we'll explore the concept of essential questions in detail, discussing in depth the features of effective essential questions, their benefits, and ways to use them in your instruction. Through strong essential questions, students can clearly identify the scopes of their inquiries and establish the frameworks of the analyses they will conduct throughout units of study. While reading this book, you'll learn how to craft effective essential questions that lead to thought-provoking reflections, interpretations, and conclusions.

◆ **Inquiry-based literature instruction is especially effective when its topics facilitate authentic connections with students' lives and with real-world issues.** To maximize the effectiveness of inquiry-based literature instruction, we strongly recommend looking for essential questions, texts, and topics that align with your students' experiences and with real-world topics that engage them. Doing so facilitates student engagement and helps them make authentic connections between the ideas and texts they discuss in class and their out-of-school lives. Duncan-Andrade and Morrell (2005) emphasize the importance of creating curricula that are relevant to students' lives; inquiry-based instruction is a meaningful and easy-to-implement way to do this.

◆ **Inquiry-based literature instruction is especially effective when it incorporates a wide range of texts.** An important feature of inquiry-based instruction is that it facilitates the use of a number of texts. By engaging students in inquiries that address thought-provoking and wide-ranging topics, we teachers create instructional contexts that naturally lend themselves to the use of a variety of texts. For example, one of the students mentioned in the book's opening vignette examined essential questions related to the challenging of gender roles; this inquiry aligned with examinations of a number of texts related to this topic. By considering a variety of works and genres related to a topic and essential question, students can reflect carefully and thoughtfully on the unit's central ideas.

Why We Decided to Write This Book

We decided to write this book to give teachers a practical, classroom-ready, and research-based resource to use when planning and enacting inquiry-based literature instruction with their students. The concept of inquiry is a significant and current one in education in general, and a number of resources have recently been published that provide educators with important overarching insights on this topic, such Krebs and Zvi's previously mentioned *The Genius Hour Guidebook* (2015) and A. J. Juliani's *Inquiry and Innovation in the Classroom: Using 20% Time, Genius Hour, and PBL to Drive Student Success* (2015). These books convey the positive effects that inquiry can have on student learning, engagement, and achievement. Given the impacts of the approaches they describe and the potential alignment between this instruction model and effective English teaching, we believe there is a need for a book that focuses specifically on inquiry-based literature instruction. Such a book, we feel, can build on existing, more general inquiry-focused texts by helping teachers apply the principles of this successful, engaging, and challenging framework to their students' interactions with works of literature.

We wrote this book to provide you, the teachers reading it, with an instructional guide that will help you understand the impact, features, and variety of implementation methods associated with inquiry-based literature instruction. As authors of this book, we have two main goals. The first is to help you understand the impact and features of literature instruction that uses essential questions and a wide range of texts and perspectives to engage students in thought-provoking inquiry. The second goal is to demonstrate how inquiry-based literature instruction can look in practice, conveying a range of ways teachers can implement it. We want for you to finish reading this book and understand the importance of inquiry-based inquiry instruction, as well as a variety of methods for putting it into action in your classroom.

What to Expect in This Book

This book is divided into four sections, each one designed to address an important aspect of inquiry-based literature instruction. The first section, which focuses on key background and contextual information, contains this Introduction and Chapters One and Two of the book, each containing insights and ideas that will help you understand the impact and usefulness of the instructional approach the book describes. Chapter One conveys the importance of inquiry, discussing in more detail the inquiry-related ideas we've introduced so far and describing in depth why and how inquiry-based instruction can help reconceptualize literature instruction. Chapter Two provides a detailed discussion of the features and significance of essential questions, conveying their key attributes and benefits. After you finish Chapter Two, you'll know what makes a question truly essential and understand how to create them for your own classroom.

The book's second section is titled "What Can Inquiry-Based Literature Instruction Look Like?" and comprises Chapters Three, Four, and Five. These three chapters provide in-depth descriptions of three inquiry-based units Sean worked on with eighth-graders. Each chapter in this section provides a discussion of the unit's instructional goals; a rationale to share with parents, students, and administrators; information on the assessments Sean's students completed; and outlines of the daily lesson plans Sean used in the unit. The projects described in these chapters convey the range of ways inquiry-based learning can take shape in the English classroom. Chapter Three is titled "An Inquiry-Driven Unit on Social Action"; in this unit, students considered the essential question "What inspires individuals to take part in social action?" Its central text was the novel *The Epic Fail of Arturo Zamora* by Pablo Cartaya; in addition to this novel, students considered a range of songs, poems, visual art, and nonfiction articles related to the essential question.

Chapter Four of the book, titled "Student-Selected Text Sets in an Inquiry-Driven Unit," examines another construction of inquiry-based instruction. It describes a unit in which eighth-graders examined the essential question "How and why do people challenge social norms?" In this unit, Sean read aloud the book *Bronx Masquerade* by Nikki Grimes, using this text as a starting point and a touchstone for the class's discussion of the focal question. In this unit, students selected independent reading books that they felt aligned with the essential question; while reading these books, the students reflected on how the information in the text helped them respond to that question. In addition to these independent reading books, students selected additional texts that they felt were relevant; specifically, students were asked to select two other texts (each representing a different genre) that they felt addressed the essential question. For example, one student in Sean's class selected the novel *Dear Martin* by Nic Stone, the poem "I Look at the World" by Langston Hughes, and Kehinde Wiley's portrait paintings; she described the connection between these works, the read-aloud book, and the unit's essential question.

Chapter Five, "Connecting Genius Hour and Inquiry Through Student-Selected Inquiries," describes an approach to inquiry-based literature instruction that incorporates even more student choice and ownership. Inspired by the student-interest-driven principles of Genius Hour (Krebs & Zvi, 2015), this form of instruction asks students to select their own essential questions and curate text sets that align with that question. (The examples discussed at the beginning of this chapter of students investigating inquiry-oriented questions and corresponding texts were created by students engaged in this instructional approach.) When Sean conducted this work with his students, he guided them through the process of deciding on an inquiry-oriented essential question that was meaningful to them and selecting a range of texts that would allow them to address that question. Sean asked his students to select three texts when conducting their inquiries—one book-length work and two texts from the genres of poetry, art, music, film, television, informational articles, or another approved option. In this chapter, we'll look closely at the instructional practices Sean used as he facilitated his students' work with this innovative and student-centered process.

After these chapters that describe how inquiry-based literature instruction can look, we'll move to Section Three of the book. This section, titled "Putting It All Together," provides important insights to consider when incorporating the instructional approach described in this book. Chapter Six, "Assessing Inquiry," describes ideas and suggestions for assessing students' inquiry-based learning. The insights in this chapter are designed to help you incorporate the principles of authentic and meaningful assessment into inquiry-based literature instruction. In Chapter Seven, "Supporting English Language Learners in Inquiry-Based Literature Instruction," we discuss how inquiry-based literature instruction is effective for facilitating English Language Learners' literacy learning and provide research-based recommendations to consider as you support English Language Learners while incorporating inquiry-based literacy instruction in your classroom. This section concludes with Chapter Eight, "Key Recommendations to Keep in Mind When Conducting Inquiry-Driven Units," in which we share important instructional tips to keep in mind when incorporating inquiry-based literature instruction into your classroom.

The book concludes with Section Four, which contains resources designed to support you in your work with inquiry-based literature instruction. The "Guide for Book Studies" in Appendix A identifies thought-provoking reflection questions and prompts to consider when using this book as a book-study text. We highly recommend engaging in a book study of this text with other teachers in your professional learning network; doing so can allow you to collaboratively discuss the ideas and practices the book describes and brainstorm ways to apply its ideas to your own instruction. Appendix B provides templates, guides, and graphic organizers you can use when planning your own inquiry-based literature instruction; these resources will help you create unit plans like those described in this book. Finally, the References section provides citation information about many valuable and informative sources that you can examine if you'd like to investigate ideas related to inquiry-based literature instruction in more detail.

By utilizing an inquiry-based approach, we English teachers can make literature instruction as engaging, effective, and thought-provoking as possible for our students. This approach facilitates deep thinking, intertextual connections, and real-world applicability. We've designed this book to give teachers a practitioner-oriented and research-based resource to use when applying inquiry-based instructional practices. Through the ideas described in this book, we can engage our students in meaningful inquiries that lead to thoughtful engagement with challenging and relevant questions. We're thrilled that you've chosen to use this book as a guide in your learning about this instructional approach. Now, let's begin our exploration of inquiry-based literature instruction!

1

The Importance of Inquiry

The idea of inquiry has gained a great deal of popularity in education because of its ability to facilitate student agency and in-depth thinking: through inquiry-based learning, students investigate complex topics and thought-provoking questions that defy simplistic answers (Lee, 2012). While this book specifically discusses inquiry-oriented study in the middle and high school English classroom, it is worth noting that inquiry-oriented teaching and learning has become popular in elementary school, middle school, high school, and college instruction (Hmelo-Silver, 2004) and plays a prominent role in a wide range of subjects, from science to the humanities (Lee, 2012). Given this range of grade levels and subject areas (as well as individual teachers' preferences), inquiry-oriented instruction can take a variety of forms. The instructional approaches described in this book focus on how to incorporate inquiry in three specific ways: designing a unit around an inquiry with a teacher-selected text, inviting students to select texts within an inquiry unit, and facilitating student inquiry during Genius Hour and other times devoted specifically to students' inquiries. Each of these methods serve as an opportunity for students to consider nuanced and complex questions. These questions can promote reflection on important societal issues and facilitate the incorporation of multiple perspectives and ideas.

Rethinking the Idea of "Unit"

In this chapter, we'll explore an approach to unit construction that goes beyond aligning each instructional unit to a single text. Specifically, we'll examine the inquiry-focused unit. Such a unit can have a central text, but also incorporates other works that conceptually relate to important topics and ideas in the book, allowing students to engage with a wide range of texts. This range of texts facilitates students' abilities to conduct inquiry into relevant topics by helping them reflect on issues raised in all of the works.

When teachers conduct inquiry-focused units, they can still address key concepts and topics related to key ideas in a work of literature, but they position that work differently: instead of the unit's central instructional goal being only to read and understand one text, the students' readings and understandings of the text becomes a way to find out more about a relevant question or idea about which they can conduct thoughtful and in-depth inquiry. We believe that this method can reconceptualize literature instruction for you and your students, because it positions *authentic, real-world questions, not specific texts* at the center of your English curriculum.

In Chapter Three, we'll look at Sean's experiences teaching a unit to an eighth-grade English class that focused on the question "What inspires individuals to take part in social action?" The central text for this unit was Pablo Cartaya's (2017) young adult novel *The Epic Fail of Arturo Zamora*. Because the unit foregrounded the inquiry question rather than a particular text, other texts could be brought in to move students toward deeper understandings about the initial question.

In addition to Cartaya's novel, Sean's students examined a wide range of other texts in this unit, addressing ideas related to social action, such as music, poetry, art, and non-fiction articles. The combination of these texts provided students with a variety of ways to consider the unit's focus of what inspires individuals to get involved in social action, contextualizing key ideas in *The Epic Fail of Arturo Zamora* with contemporary and historical connections to important concepts in the text. In this unit, the novel was only an entry point for the students' inquiry into the idea of getting involved in social action and provided a touchstone for the class to continually refer back to as we examined interdisciplinary perspectives. As the students reacted to and reflected on the music, art, poetry, and non-fiction articles that were embedded in the unit, they used *The Epic Fail of Arturo Zamora* as a point of comparison that helped them engage with each text and enter into dialogue with each other.

The units described in Chapters Four and Five also convey the possibilities and potential of inquiry-based literature instruction. For example, the combination of a whole-class read aloud text and student-selected independent reading texts appropriate to a unit's inquiry topic, as described in Chapter Four, reveal a way to align the practices of independent reading with inquiry-based learning. Similarly, the student-driven inquiries discussed in Chapter Five combine independent reading with Genius Hour's student-interest-driven orientation. Given the significance of independent reading to effective literacy instruction identified in research-based documents such as the NCTE Position Statement on Independent Reading (NCTE, 2019) and peer-reviewed journal articles (such as Brooks & Frankel's 2019 article "Authentic Choice: A Plan for Independent Reading in a Restrictive Instructional Setting"), it is noteworthy that inquiry-based literacy instruction aligns well with independent reading practices.

The Affordances of Inquiry-Focused Units

As fellow English teachers, we think that inquiry-focused units will allow you to reconceptualize your literature instruction in multiple ways—all while keeping curriculum standards in mind. First, they provide opportunities for you to have students engage with multiple genres at the same time. Too often, we see poetry only being taught in April, or teachers saving a nonfiction piece for the nonfiction unit. We believe firmly that inquiry-focused units can create spaces for you to ask your students to read and analyze myriad print and non-print genres simultaneously. Curriculum standards related to reading particular text genres can be met in the context of students' inquiries. For example, Sean's students examined songs, poems, art, and nonfiction texts as they worked to answer the inquiry posed.

Second, mimicking real-world, organic research in which people look to multiple sources (e.g., TV, social media, art, newspapers, fiction texts, nonfiction articles), inquiry-focused units can help your students meet curriculum standards concerning research throughout the academic year, not just during "The Research Unit." Opportunities for helping students locate and assess texts related to inquiries abound as students engage in inquiry-focused units. In the unit described in Chapter Three, for example, students not only read a nonfiction article but were also asked to find and bring in a nonfiction article that related to the inquiry.

And, third, we believe that inquiry-oriented approaches to English instruction are particularly effective ways to incorporate a range of perspectives into the classroom—thereby increasing the types of representation in the curriculum—because they focus on important topics and questions that are best addressed by examining a number of points of view. Because of this, inquiry naturally lends itself to the inclusion of a range of perspectives and ideas, especially when compared to units that focus on a singular text or author. No matter what text is used in a single-text unit, that unit is limited in its perspectives and in its diversity of representation. By contrast, an inquiry-focused unit that addresses a complex and nuanced question best answered by examining a number of points of view and perspectives provides teachers with an authentic and organic opportunity to incorporate a wide range of texts. For example, the unit that Sean conducted with an eighth-grade English class on what inspires individuals to take part in social action facilitated discussion on more than the unit's central novel, Pablo Cartaya's *The Epic Fail of Arturo Zamora*. Since the students were engaged in an inquiry about a multifaceted topic that relates to key aspects of the book, they were able to thoughtfully reflect on the novel as well as other texts that address the inquiry topic.

Student Reactions to Inquiry

Throughout the inquiry-based units described in this book, Sean asked his students for their thoughts on the inquiry-oriented approach. The students' comments illustrated that they enjoyed the opportunity to engage in inquiry that went beyond a single-text focus, that they learned a great deal from the multiple perspectives included in the unit, and that they felt this unit incorporated diverse points of view in ways that other instructional approaches they had experienced did not. The comments below convey these themes:

> I really liked [how] we talked about a bunch of texts that were related to the theme, like the songs, poems, and paintings. Usually in English class we just read one book, but in this project, we talked about a bunch of texts that all related to the theme, not just one book.

> What I learned the most from was all of the different ways we looked at what inspires people to take part in social action. Because of this, I feel like I know a lot about all the different ways people get inspired to take part in social action.

> This was really different—in a good way!—from what I'm used to in English because of all the different points of view. All of the different things you brought in for us to think about had different kinds of points of view. These points of view made what we did a lot more diverse than if you didn't bring in all of those different things.

> Being able to select my own inquiry topic was awesome. I could pick a topic I care about and find a bunch of texts related to it. Before this year, I'd never done inquiry in English [class] and I definitely never picked my own topic to study like this!

I loved how we could pick our own books and other kinds of things, like songs, poems, and art that had to with the inquiry. It was like we had a lot more say in how we learned. Thanks!

Final Thoughts on the Power of Inquiry-Focused Units

Throughout this book, we'll consider specific ways to put inquiry-focused units into practice in the middle and high school English classroom. Before we get into those details, let's consider some final thoughts to keep in mind related to the power and significance of diversity-focused inquiry units:

- ◆ Inquiry-focused units ask students to conduct an inquiry into a topic or concept that connects to their world—one that addresses the perspectives of a variety of individuals, especially those not typically represented in the literary canon.
- ◆ Inquiry-focused units can have a central text, but also incorporate other works that conceptually relate to important topics and ideas in the book.
- ◆ Inquiry-focused units that include a range of texts facilitate students' abilities to conduct inquiry into relevant topics by helping them reflect on issues raised in all of the works.
- ◆ Inquiry-focused units in the English classroom are particularly effective ways to incorporate a range of perspectives in the classroom—thereby increasing the types of representation in the curriculum—because they focus on important topics and questions that are best addressed by examining a number of points of view.
- ◆ Inquiry-focused units that address complex and nuanced questions best answered by examining a number of points of view and perspectives provide teachers with an authentic and organic opportunity to incorporate a wide range of texts.

2

Inquiry and Essential Questions

In this chapter, we'll explore one of the most important and fundamental components of inquiry units: the creation of essential questions. The information we'll share in this chapter will help you understand key concepts related to essential questions and how you can put these ideas into action in your classroom. We'll describe what essential questions are, why they are important, and how they are especially meaningful in the context of today's classrooms.

What Are Essential Questions?

It is our experience—in our own classrooms and in those that we have observed over the years—that English teachers become particularly excited about the questions we ask our students. As Jay McTighe and Grant Wiggins (2013) articulate in their book *Essential Questions: Opening Doors to Student Understanding*, teachers pose questions to their students all the time. We can all probably agree with Judith A. Langer's (2011) idea that "the literary experience *requires* the raising of questions" (p. 69). Creating rich, engaging, and meaningful classroom experiences for your students, however, requires more than just any question. It is, of course, essential questions that we believe ignite students' learning and ways of thinking about texts and their lives.

We use Wiggins and McTighe's (2005) definition of *essential question*:

A question that lies at the heart of a subject or a curriculum (as opposed to either being trivial or leading), and promotes inquiry and uncoverage of a subject. Essential questions thus do not yield a single straightforward answer (as a leading question does) but produce different plausible responses, about which thoughtful and knowledgeable people may disagree.

(p. 342)

McTighe and Wiggins (2013) ask teachers to think about the differences between these two questions: "Who is Maggie's best friend in the story?" and "Who is a true friend?" (p. 1). Whereas the first question requires a one-word answer, the correct name of Maggie's friend, the second question requires students to ponder deeply the characteristics of someone who is considered a friend. There is a certain level of cognitive horsepower needed for the second question, which does not have a predetermined answer. In addition, the idea of who a true friend is continues to be a question for most of us throughout our lives.

McTighe and Wiggins (2013) offer seven characteristics of essential questions. They suggest that an essential question meets most or all of the following characteristics:

- ◆ is open-ended;
- ◆ is thought-provoking;
- ◆ calls for higher-order thinking;
- ◆ points toward important, transferable ideas;
- ◆ raises additional questions and sparks further inquiry;
- ◆ requires support and justification, not just an answer;
- ◆ and recurs over time, or can be revisited frequently.

(p. 3)

In her book *The Essential Questions Handbook Grades 4–8*, Carolyn McConnell (2011) shares what she thinks of as an essential question: "The best questions for stimulating student thinking are the ones that cannot be answered easily. In fact, the best questions often have no answer—at least, no one 'correct' answer" (p. 5). In her *Mapping the Big Picture: Integrating Curriculum & Assessment K-12*, Heidi Hayes Jacobs's (1997) juxtaposes the objective "The student will look at the three branches of government as organized in the Constitution" with the following question: "How is the Constitution the backbone structure of America?" (p. 26). Whereas the first sentence articulates narrowly the goal of enabling students to name the government's three branches, the second question provides students an opportunity to think deeply about a concept that becomes broader than a single lesson about the three branches. Jacobs (1997) shares that essential questions allow teachers to "upgrade" their plans. These amped-up curricula provide spaces for students to engage deeply in worthwhile inquiries that transcend isolated standards and matter enormously to the world.

Why Are Essential Questions Important?

Many of us think fondly of our college literature courses with classmates who were eagerly ready to discuss texts and remember being drawn to teaching English because of how texts helped us consider the bigger issues in the world and make sense of our lives. In our work as teacher educators, we often ask our preservice teachers about their experiences in literature courses in high school and college. Sometimes we hear that students were nervous to share their ideas because they knew the teacher had "the" answer in mind. We think essential questions can help with this oft-perceived notion that the teacher knows "the" answer to every question. Essential questions are important because they allow you to create opportunities for your students to grapple with authentic, challenging questions that do not have simple (or sometimes any) answers as they develop understandings and a voice.

Essential questions encourage students to consider responses to questions that do not have predetermined answers. They honor the belief that inquiry is the true purpose of learning (McTighe & Wiggins, 2013), that we want our students to continue asking questions when they leave our classrooms. In her book *Envisioning Literature: Literary Understanding and Literature Instruction*, Judith A. Langer (2011) shares that questions are an essential component to one's experiences with texts. For Langer, exploring literature is part of what she coins envisionment building. She defines *envisionment* as "the world of understanding a person has at a given point in time" (p. 10). As we read, we move into an envisionment, move through the envisionment, step out and rethink what we know, step out and objectify the experience, and leave an envisionment and go beyond. Langer suggests, "Through literature, students learn to explore possibilities and consider options; they gain connectedness and seek vision" (p. 2). As they encourage students to build and reconsider their envisionments, well-written questions have the ability to create powerful learning experiences that encourage students to ponder some of the magnificent questions of our time as they contemplate issues grander than themselves and find connections between the texts they read in your class and the world in which they live. And they continue to ponder these questions—perhaps altering their answer multiple times.

Essential questions are important because they allow you to move beyond coverage and toward a curriculum that engages students in the depth and relevance of the texts being explored. McTighe and Wiggins (2013) ask teachers to contemplate a more traditional curriculum:

> If the content you are expected to teach represents "answers," then what questions were being asked by the people who came up with those answers? This conceptual move offers a useful strategy both for seeing a link between content standards and important questions and for coming up with ways of engaging students in the very kind of thinking that is required to truly understand the content.
>
> (p. 4)

McTighe and Wiggins (2013) posit that when posed with essential questions, "learners are engaged in *uncovering* the depth and richness of a topic that might otherwise be obscured by simply *covering* it" (p. 3). This transformed view of how we see our curriculum—and the questions within it—can help students build transferrable skills and ways of thinking.

Because they are tackling meaningful inquiries, students who are working on answering essential questions are engaged in critical thinking and perspective-building. McTighe and Wiggins (2013) urge teachers to consider how essential questions differ from other types of questions that hook (e.g., " 'Can what you eat and drink help prevent zits?' " [p. 12]), lead (e.g., " 'What is seven times six?' " [p. 11]), or guide (e.g., ' "Is this sentence punctuated properly?' " [p. 11]) students. Questions that just hook may generate interest but not deep engagement, questions that lead do not stimulate inquiry, and questions that guide expect students to arrive at a predetermined answer.

The type of essential questions McTighe and Wiggins encourage are those composed "for students to continuously examine so as to 'come to an understanding' of key ideas and processes" (p. 14). As students come to these understandings, there are many possibilities for interdisciplinary connections, allowing students to consider how myriad people across a range of disciplines think about a particular topic (McTighe & Wiggins, 2013). One way to consider whether our essential questions are effective is for us to think to ourselves: *Does the answer to this question matter to me? Does the answer to this question have implications in the greater world? Do I want to spend several weeks devoted to the pursuit of an answer to this question?*

Creating essential questions allows you to reframe your curriculum in a way that honors student voices because students gain autonomy and agency in a curriculum designed around essential questions. As they articulate their answer, they are revealing to you and to themselves that they can offer new ideas and responses that are valid. As McTighe and Wiggins (2013) suggest, "Expert knowledge is the result of inquiry, argument, and difference of opinion; the best questions point to hard-won big ideas that we want learners to come to understand" (pp. 4–5). As they encourage metacognition (McTighe & Wiggins, 2013), essential questions can help you move your students toward grander, sophisticated understandings about the texts they read and the world in which they live. McTighe and Wiggins (2013) consider essential questions central parts of a curriculum that will allow students to "develop and deepen [their] understanding of important ideas and processes so that they can transfer their learning within and outside school" (p. 4). Essential questions create opportunities for students to not only consider the text or texts at hand deeply but also how the text or texts relate to the world beyond what is contained within the book's pages and the four walls of the classroom—to their lives and the lives of those around them. This is exactly why so many of us came into the English classroom in the first place: to help students connect what they were reading to their lives and the world around them—not to identify an obscure literary element on a standardized test.

Most importantly, however, essential questions are important because they are *real*. They are, as McTighe and Wiggins (2013) say, "alive" (p. 8). They encourage students to think deeply about challenging questions that do not have simple or "right" answers and permit you to model the lifelong skills of questioning, of wondering, of inquiring about one's world (McTighe & Wiggins, 2013). The best essential questions are those that people outside of the English classroom might discuss: "a question is alive in a subject if we really engage with it, if it seems genuine and relevant to us, and if it helps us gain a more systematic and deep understanding of what we are learning" (p. 8). They help students discuss topics that are meaningful and relevant to their lives, extending students' thinking and understanding beyond an isolated lesson concept or singular text, urging students to wrestle with myriad questions that exist within texts but also in the real world. Essential questions give students in your English classroom the opportunity to engage with the multiple answers to some of the most pertinent questions in our local, national, or global communities.

Why Do Essential Questions Matter in Today's Classrooms?

We believe essential questions work particularly well in the context of the variety of perspectives present in today's English classrooms. They provide a means by which to engage students in issues that are important to them. The International Literacy Association's (ILA, 2019) *Children's Rights to Read* articulates, "Children have the right to read texts that mirror their experiences and languages, provide windows into the lives of others, and open doors into our diverse world." This makes the inclusion of essential questions in the English classroom paramount.

Essential questions matter in today's classrooms because they allow today's students to consider deeply answers to questions that matter in their lives and in their communities. In her seminal work *Literature as Exploration*, Louise Rosenblatt (1968) writes that a text alone has no meaning. For Rosenblatt, it is the reader who brings meaning to the text. The making of meaning is "a *transaction* between the reader and the text" (p. 35). She eloquently writes:

> Someone else can read the newspaper or a scientific work for us and summarize it acceptably. But no one can read a poem for us. The reader of the poem must have the experience himself.
>
> (p. 33)

We believe that using essential questions within a curriculum allows students in the English classroom to experience the text themselves, to create meaning from the text. Through the meaningful, real, authentic questions posed, students are able to consider texts in the context of the viewpoints they bring into the classroom.

Essential questions allow students to deepen their understanding of complex topics as they relate personally to the topics at hand. In the English classroom, essential questions can help students wrestle with the "big ideas that great literature explores—the universal themes of human condition underneath the more obvious peculiarities of personality or culture—and thus can help us gain experience into our own experiences" (McTighe & Wiggins, 2013, p. 5). Rudine Sims Bishop's (1990) piece articulates that books can be windows, mirrors, and sliding glass doors for readers. They can reflect who we are as people, provide us insight into others' worlds, or leave us changed. Interestingly, McTighe and Wiggins (2013) articulate a similar concept about the power of essential questions: "The questions thus serve as doorways and lenses through which learners can better see and explore the key concepts, themes, issues, and problems that reside within the content" (p. 5). Too often, however, we have focused on the windows and mirrors aspect of Bishop's (1990) work, emphasizing less the powerful sliding glass door component (Johnson, Koss, & Martinez, 2018).

Essential questions provide grand opportunities to help student readers see texts as sliding glass doors. Books that are most likely to become sliding glass doors often have complex characters who engage in action for change

(Johnson et al., 2018). Johnson et al. (2018) write, "When books ignite readers' questions, they may move readers through sliding glass doors. These books trouble readers' thinking and prod them to consider what they might do to take action" (p. 573). Johnson et al. (2018) provide several qualities to look for when selecting books that open opportunities for sliding glass doors, but the one that most relates to our work with essential questions is having characters who interrogate the world around them. And certainly, one could argue that many texts have characters who do this. We can indeed think of a multitude of canonical texts and contemporary middle grades and young adult titles that do this!

Reflecting the voices within our classrooms, essential questions around texts offer grand opportunities for students to engage in questions that truly matter in the world. Essential questions designed to help students think about the diversity in their world have the potential power to move students to consider what changes they can make to make our world a better place. Seeing how different characters respond differently to a similar situation may alter your students' answers to the initial essential question posed. We know essential questions can help you help your students understand that their ideas, their perspectives, their stories, and their voices matter and that they have the ability to advocate for change in their communities.

Section Two

What Can Inquiry-Based Literature Instruction Look Like?

3

An Inquiry-Driven Unit on Social Action

In this chapter, we'll look at the first of the three inquiry-based units described in this section of the book. As explained in the book's introduction, these three units represent different ways that inquiry-driven instruction can look in the English classroom. The unit described here, which Sean taught to an eighth-grade English class, focused on the essential question "What inspires individuals to take part in social action?" Its central text was the novel *The Epic Fail of Arturo Zamora* by Pablo Cartaya; in addition to this novel, the unit also asked students to consider a range of songs, poems, visual art, and non-fiction articles.

We'll examine that unit by considering several of its components and attributes. First, we'll unpack the unit's essential question, its significance, and how the question facilitated the use of a range of texts. After that, we'll look closely at the unit's text set, including key features of each of the pieces students analyzed for the unit and how each aligns with the essential question. Next, we'll examine the rationale that Sean shared with administrators, students, and families before teaching the unit to an eighth-grade class. Following that, we'll check out the assessment Sean implemented with his eighth-graders at the completion of this unit. Then, we'll see outlines of the daily lesson plans used in the unit. Finally, we'll consider key takeaway ideas that you can connect to your own instruction.

The purpose of this chapter is to illustrate one approach that an inquiry-oriented unit can take; as you'll see throughout the chapter, the unit described here utilizes a contemporary young-adult novel and a wide range of other texts from a variety of genres and time periods to help students think about and ultimately respond to the unit's essential question. As you examine this example unit, we encourage you to think about how you might construct similarly structured inquiry-oriented units with your students. While you can certainly teach this unit to your students in its current form, we also suggest that, as you read the details of this unit, you think about one or more key essential questions that might especially engage your students. After you've identified that question or those questions, we recommend identifying a central novel that you believe would engage and challenge your students while helping them reflect on the essential question or questions. Once you've thought about this novel, you can begin to think of additional texts that can work in concert with the novel to help your students consider the essential question(s) in nuanced and informed ways. Let's get started by looking at the essential question Sean selected for this unit and the thought process associated with it.

Essential Question

The essential question that guided this unit was "What inspires individuals to take part in social action?" Sean selected this question for a variety of reasons. First, the question was of high interest to the students to whom the unit was taught. Many students in this class were concerned with social issues, having attended a number of protests, rallies, and demonstrations in Virginia (where the unit was taught) and in Washington, DC. Since the students often raised questions and shared insights in class about social action, Sean wanted to capitalize on their interests.

In addition, the unit's broad scope facilitated the use of a number of texts, which allowed students to consider an important issue from a wide range of perspectives. The varying perspectives and insights provided by the range of texts in this unit helped students develop nuanced responses to the unit's essential question. When he introduced the essential question at the beginning of the unit, Sean explained to the students the importance of using a variety of texts to help them respond to the question. "Our essential question, 'What inspires individuals to take part in social action?' is a broad one," he told them, "and it has a lot of different components and possible explanations. Because of this, we're going to look at a really wide range of texts to help us understand the question and create thoughtful, well-informed responses to it."

The fact that the unit's essential question lent itself to a wide range of texts also helped Sean align the unit with key instructional standards. The Virginia Standards of Learning for eighth grade call for students to "read and analyze a variety of fictional texts, literary nonfiction, poetry, and drama" (VA SOL 8.5) and "read, comprehend, and analyze a variety of nonfiction texts" (VA SOL 8.6). In addition, the Common Core State Standards explain that students "should read widely and deeply from among a broad range of high-quality, increasingly challenging literary and informational texts" (2010). The wide-ranging focus and correspondingly broad essential question of this unit facilitated students' interactions with the variety of texts addressed in these standards.

As you craft inquiry-based units like this one to use with your students, we encourage you to reflect on the standards in your state and how they align with this type of unit. We've found that many current and rigorous state standards encourage the kinds of in-depth analysis facilitated by inquiry-based units. For example, the Colorado Academic Standards for eighth-grade reading, writing, and communication specifically cite inquiry as a component of effective instruction and call for students to read and interpret texts from a wide range of genres (Colorado Department of Education, 2020). While details of specific state standards vary, the analytical work students do in inquiry-based learning will help them succeed in a wide range of academic and real-world situations, as the skills associated with reflecting on an essential question and interpreting a variety of sources can be widely applied. Now that we've considered the strengths of this unit's essential questions and the way these questions align with a variety of texts, skills, and standards, let's check out the texts featured in the unit.

Text Set

In this unit, students engaged with texts representative of a range of genres, perspectives, and experiences. While all of these works connected with the essential question—"What inspires individuals to take part in social action?"—they provided students with a number of ways of engaging with the key ideas embedded in the unit's focus. In this section, we'll look at the texts used in this unit, important features of each one, and how each work aligns with the unit's essential question. As the descriptions here indicate, the unit's text set contains a number of genres, such as a novel, songs (or song excerpts), poetry, artwork, and nonfiction articles.

Novel

◆ *The Epic Fail of Arturo Zamora* by Pablo Cartaya. This novel describes 13-year-old Arturo's experience trying to save his family's restaurant from a land developer and his sources of inspiration, such as letters written by his deceased grandfather and the works of Cuban revolutionary poet José Martí. It represented the central text for the unit—students read it throughout the unit and used it as an initial point-of-reference regarding the essential question. The social activism in this text is both specific and generalizable: although the particular actions in which Arturo engages are local to a certain situation and context, many aspects of them can be connected to other examples of social action.

Songs (or Song Excerpts)

◆ "My Shot" from the musical *Hamilton*. This song, which features multiple characters in *Hamilton* discussing their desires to fight for America's independence, provided an excellent entry point for students as they began to consider similarities and differences in the reasons individuals engage in social action.

◆ "The General" by Dispatch. This song describes a military general's changing perspective on war. Before a significant battle, he explains that he has thought about the members of the opposition as individuals and encourages his troops to choose not to participate in the battle. This text provided students with an example of social action in which a character adopts a new perspective.

◆ "Keep Ya Head Up" by 2Pac. In this song, 2Pac calls for men to be respectful of women and discusses how disrespectful behavior towards women has a negative impact on society in a variety of ways. While discussing this important issue, 2Pac also comments on other issues of inequality. This text was very well-received by the students—they appreciated 2Pac's social consciousness and his advocacy-oriented perspective. Students made a variety of connections to this song throughout the unit.

◆ "Hero" by Nas. In this song, Nas discusses his experiences challenging social norms and being an inspiring role model for others who are trying to achieve their dreams. He addresses problems with corporate greed and explains how he views his music and status as vehicles for making a difference in the world. Students made very insightful connections between the ideas in this song and the protagonist of *The Epic Fail of Arturo Zamora*.

Poetry

◆ "I Have A White Rose to Tend" by José Martí. This poem, which is included in the book *The Epic Fail of Arturo Zamora* and plays a role in Arturo's coming-of-age process, addresses the idea of being consistently compassionate and kind towards all. The students thoughtfully considered how the commitment toward kindness and compassion discussed in this poem related to the unit's essential question, reflecting on how one's social action is often inspired by that individual's focus on all people being treated fairly.

◆ "Still I Rise" by Maya Angelou. This poem's message of hopefulness and persistence in the face of oppression can facilitate important connections to the topic of why individuals take part in social action. The students discussed how the poem's speaker responds to discrimination and mistreatment with confidence and resilience; they compared this speaker's mentality with other examples they examined throughout the unit.

◆ "Wage Peace" by Judyth Hill. This poem provides an excellent action of a text that can inspire social action. The piece carefully contrasts desolate and hopeful images and calls for the reader to work for and celebrate peace and beauty. The students found this to be an especially powerful text when reflecting on what the goals of social action can look like.

Artwork

◆ *Rage, Flower Thrower* by Banksy. The piece depicts a black and white drawing of a man with a covered face and backwards hat who is positioned to throw an object; his body language suggests he is prepared to use a great deal of force in his throw. The item to be thrown is a bouquet of flowers—the only component of the image in color. This powerful image provides a great visual representation of the impact of social action.

◆ *Face 2 Face Project* by JR and Marco. In this piece, the artists photographed Israelis and Palestinians making silly and smiling faces and placed the photos in Israeli and Palestinian cities, conveying the message that all individuals share the same human emotions. This artwork led to interesting conversations among the students because the art itself was an example of a social action meant to promote empathy.

◆ *For Some, It's Mt. Everest* by the American Disabilities Association. This piece is a photograph of Mt. Everest placed on a set of public stairs by the American Disabilities Association. On one stair is the text "For some, it's Mt. Everest." The stair underneath that one contains the text "Help build more handicap facilities." Directly underneath is another stair that contains the name and logo of the

American Disabilities Association. Students responded thoughtfully to this piece, describing how it can provide important motivation for social action.

Nonfiction Articles

◆ "7 Times in History When Students Turned to Activism" by Maggie Astor. This article, published by the *New York Times* in 2018, discusses a variety of examples of students and other young people engaging in social activism, ranging from 1960 to present. The examples in this article provided excellent examples for students to reflect on as they considered the unit's essential question. In addition, these examples facilitated insightful connections to other texts in the unit.

◆ Student-selected nonfiction articles. In addition to Astor's piece, Sean asked all of the students to bring in a nonfiction article of their choice that described an example of social action. They selected a range of topics, including pieces about Colin Kaepernick's activism, the United States' Women's Soccer Team's fight for equity, musicians' social actions, television shows and films that have been forward-thinking on important issues, current and historical political protests, and other excellent examples. By bringing in these articles, students were able to make personal additions to the unit's text set and think further about the essential question.

Rationale

The following is the rationale that Sean shared with the administrators at the school where he taught this unit. In addition, Sean shared it with the students and their families so that everyone involved had a complete understanding of the key attributes and benefits of this unit. We encourage you to create rationales for your inquiry-based units in order to convey to administrators, students, and families the components of these units and the positive impacts they can have on students. We've provided more information on unit rationales in the "Key Takeaway Ideas" section later in this chapter.

This document describes the unit that Sean Ruday will be working on with his eighth-grade English class. It provides a rationale for the unit by identifying and describing four of its key aspects: 1) the unit's focus, 2) the unit's key attributes, 3) the unit's connection to educational objectives, and 4) the unit's relevance to students' needs. By reading this document, you'll gain an understanding of the unit's most important features and strengths.

The Unit's Focus

This unit centers on the essential question "What inspires individuals to take part in social action?" Students will reflect on and think critically about this question; their responses to this question will be guided by their individual experiences and ideas, their interpretations of the texts we read as a class, other texts they select independently, and insights they develop through talking with peers during class discussions. The goal of the unit is for students to use a diverse array of texts to respond to this question in a way that illustrates their understandings of the texts and how those texts connect to the essential question.

The Unit's Key Attributes

There are two key attributes of this unit that align with its essential question: the texts with which students will engage and the final assessment that students will complete at its conclusion. First, a description of the texts: in this unit, students will work with a variety of texts, all of which will help them reflect on and think carefully about the essential question. The central text for this unit young adult novel is *The Epic Fail of Arturo Zamora* by Pablo Cartaya, which describes 13-year-old Arturo's experience trying to save his family's restaurant from a land developer and his sources of inspiration, such as letters written by his deceased grandfather and the works of Cuban revolutionary poet José Martí. In addition to Cartaya's novel, students will examine a wide range of other texts addressing ideas related to social action, such as music, poetry, art, and non-fiction articles. The musical texts are the full versions or excerpts from the songs "My Shot" from the musical *Hamilton*, "The General" by Dispatch, "Keep Ya Head Up" by 2Pac, and "Hero" by Nas (all lyrics shared will be school-appropriate, "radio-edited" versions). The poetry in the unit is "I Have A White Rose to Tend" by José Martí (which is featured in *The Epic Fail of Arturo Zamora*), "Still I Rise" by Maya Angelou, and "Wage Peace" by Judyth Hill. The works of art to be discussed are *Flower Thrower* by Banksy, the *Face 2 Face Project* by JR and Marco, and *For Some, It's Mt. Everest*, an advertisement by the American Disabilities Association in which subway-station stairs are painted with a picture of Mt. Everest to raise awareness of disability and accessibility-related issues. Regarding non-fiction articles, Sean will share the piece "7 Times in History When Students Turned to Activism" by Maggie Astor (published by *The New York Times* in 2018) and will then ask students to bring in non-fiction articles of their choosing about social issues and the ways people get involved in them. The combination of these texts will provide students with a variety of ways to consider the unit's focus of what inspires individuals to get involved in social action, contextualizing key ideas in *The Epic Fail of Arturo Zamora* with contemporary and historical connections to important concepts in the text.

The assessment that students will complete at the conclusion of the unit asks them to work individually to write a reflective essay that answers the unit's essential question. In this reflection, students will identify four texts that they believe connect to the essential question and use those texts to support their responses. One of these texts must be the novel *The Epic Fail of Arturo Zamora* by Pablo Cartaya that we will read as a class. Two texts must be other works that we will read together as a class during this unit. The final text will be one that was not assigned to students: it will be another text of any genre that the student believes will help answer the essential question. Students will cite these sources directly in their reflections and describe how the texts inform their thinking regarding their responses to the essential question. The recommended length of this reflective essay is three to four pages.

The Unit's Connection to Educational Objectives

This unit closely aligns with challenging, forward-thinking educational objectives that are designed to ensure students are able to think carefully and analytically about a variety of texts. Students' experiences in this unit analyzing a range of texts and using evidence from those various texts to support their interpretations will closely align with the text-dependent questions reflected in the 2017 Virginia English Standards of Learning [*Note to readers of this book: this unit was taught at a school in Virginia*]. In text-dependent questions, students read texts of different genres (such as a novel excerpt and a non-fiction article) that address the same theme and answer questions that require them to analyze the works. In addition, the learning activities in this unit align with a number of Virginia Grade Eight Standards of Learning, especially:

> VA SOL 8.5: The student will read and analyze a variety of fictional texts, literary nonfiction, poetry, and drama.
> VA SOL 8.6: The student will read, comprehend, and analyze a variety of nonfiction texts.
> VA SOL 8.7: The student will write in a variety of forms to include narrative, expository, persuasive, and reflective with an emphasis on expository and persuasive writing.
>
> (Virginia Department of Education, 2017)

It is also worth noting that the features of this unit align with the recommendations of the Common Core State Standards, which assert "To build a foundation for college and career readiness, students must read widely and deeply from among a broad range of high-quality, increasingly challenging literary and informational texts" (2010). These standards identify the benefits of students reading texts of varying genres and those that represent a wide range of cultures and time periods (Common Core State Standards Initiative, 2010). Students' experiences in this unit analyzing a wide range of texts that embody diverse perspectives will prepare them for multiple measures of academic success. Common Core State Standards for eighth grade that are especially relevant to this unit are listed here:

◆ CCSS.ELA-LITERACY.W.8.1.B: Support claim(s) with logical reasoning and relevant evidence, using accurate, credible sources and demonstrating an understanding of the topic or text.
◆ CCSS.ELA-LITERACY.W.8.4: Produce clear and coherent writing in which the development, organization, and style are appropriate to task, purpose, and audience.
◆ CCSS.ELA-LITERACY.W.8.9: Draw evidence from literary or informational texts to support analysis, reflection, and research.
◆ CCSS.ELA-LITERACY.RL.8.1: Cite the textual evidence that most strongly supports an analysis of what the text says explicitly as well as inferences drawn from the text.
◆ CCSS.ELA-LITERACY.RL.8.2: Determine a theme or central idea of a text and analyze its development over the course of the text, including its relationship to the characters, setting, and plot; provide an objective summary of the text.
◆ CCSS.ELA-LITERACY.RL.8.3: Analyze how particular lines of dialogue or incidents in a story or drama propel the action, reveal aspects of a character, or provoke a decision.
◆ CCSS.ELA-LITERACY.RL.8.5: Compare and contrast the structure of two or more texts and analyze how the differing structure of each text contributes to its meaning and style.

(Common Core State Standards Initiative, 2010)

[*Note to readers of this book: As you create your own unit rationales, consider the standards that are specific to your educational context. As discussed earlier in this chapter, inquiry-based instruction aligns with rigorous standards currently used in a variety of states, whether those are the Common Core State Standards or state-specific standards.*]

The Unit's Relevance to Students' Needs

In addition to its alignment with state and national standards, this unit also has a great deal of relevance to students. There are three primary ways this unit relates to students' academic and societal needs, all of which are listed and described below:

1. The unit can help students understand social activism.

   Social activism has played an important role in American and world history and continues to figure prominently in today's society. In addition, it has shaped many significant literary texts that our students will likely encounter in high school, college, and beyond. This unit can help students develop a deeper understanding of the ideas associated with social activism; this awareness will help them engage thoughtfully with academic texts and with the world around them.

2. The unit can promote an appreciation of diverse perspectives.

   An important feature of this unit is the wide range of texts it incorporates and the diverse perspectives represented in those texts. Through their experiences with this unit, students will engage with texts created by individuals from varying cultures, backgrounds, and identities. By interacting with and thinking about these texts, students can develop an increased appreciation of diverse perspectives. Such an appreciation can further enhance students' empathy and their abilities to examine complex issues from a variety of points of view.

3. The unit can help students apply academic skills to real-world situations.

   One of the great benefits of this unit is that the ideas they learn and the material with which they engage is not just applicable to the classroom: the skills students learn in this unit also connect to real-world situations. After learning about social activism and thinking about the value of approaching a situation from multiple perspectives, students will be able to make connections to their out-of-school lives. In addition, this unit will ask students to apply the critical-thinking strategies they learn in school to texts they may encounter outside of school, such as songs and information about current events. Through this unit, students will see that critical reading and thinking skills are just as important outside the classroom as in it.

Sean is very excited to work with the students on this unit! He feels it represents the best practices of English instruction and has the potential to benefit our students in a number of important ways. He is happy to talk further about it and encourages you to contact him at sean.ruday@gmail.com with any questions or comments.

Assessment

This section contains the assessment that Sean's students completed at the end of this unit. It contains the assessment description Sean distributed to his students and the rubric he used when evaluating students' works. As discussed in depth in the assessment description, students were asked to write a reflection that addressed the unit's essential question, using four texts: The Epic Fail of Arturo Zamora, *two other texts that the class read together, and one other student-selected text that was not part of the unit's assigned text set. When assessing your students' works on inquiry-based units, we encourage you to ask students to reflect on the essential question in ways that incorporate student choice and a variety of perspectives and to clearly communicate the expectations and assessment tools to students. We've provided more information on unit assessments in the "Key Takeaway Ideas" section later in this chapter and in Chapter Six, "Assessing Inquiry."*

Assessment Description Distributed to Students

As you know, our current unit addresses the question "What inspires individuals to take part in social action?" For our assessment on this unit, you will write a reflection that answers this question. In this reflection, you will identify four texts that you think connect to the unit's essential question and use them to support your response. One of these texts must be the novel *The Epic Fail of Arturo Zamora* by Pablo Cartaya that we read as a class. Two texts must be other works that we read together as a class during this unit. The final text will be one that was not assigned as part of this unit: it will be another text that you think helps you answer the essential question. It can be any genre—a book (fiction or nonfiction), a song, a piece of art, an article, a poem, or another for which you can make an effective case. You will need to cite these sources directly in your reflection and describe how they inform your thinking regarding your response to our essential question. (You will also cite them in a Works Cited page following the reflection.) The recommended length of your reflection is three to four typed pages in Times New Roman, double-spaced, not including the Works Cited page. I will confer with each of you regarding your response topics and text choices. I am happy to answer any questions you have and am very excited to see what you create!

Assessment Rubric

"WHAT INSPIRES INDIVIDUALS TO TAKE PART IN SOCIAL ACTION?"

Unit Assessment Rubric

Criteria	1	2	3	4	Feedback
Insights • Does the author provide thoughtful insights on what inspires individuals to take part in social action? • Are these insights clear, specific, and detailed? • Do the author's points convey a deep and nuanced understanding of what inspires individuals to take part in social action?					
Textual support • Are the author's insights supported with specific and detailed connections to relevant texts that align with the assignment parameters? • Does the author effectively communicate the relationship between these texts and the unit's essential question? • Is it clear that the author has carefully analyzed these texts with the unit's essential question in mind?					
Organization • Is the paper clearly organized? • Are paragraphs used in the paper's organization? • Is it clear when the author moves from one "train of thought" to another?					
Mechanics • Does the writing utilize proper mechanics? • Does it demonstrate an understanding of proper punctuation? • Are sentences clear and representative of complete thoughts? • Is capitalization used at appropriate times?					

1-criteria not met;   2-criteria partially met;   3-criteria met;   4-criteria exceeded

Total score:
Overall feedback:

Daily Lesson Plans

This section contains outlines of the daily lesson plans Sean used in this unit. Each day's description lists the day's focus, any work done before class, the main learning activities, and key state and national standards addressed in the day's lesson. These lesson plan outlines are meant to provide an overarching model for how an inquiry-based unit that uses a whole-class text can look. We encourage you to use these plan outlines as inspiration and guidance as you plan similar units for your students!

Day One: Introduction of Essential Question

Key Learning Activities:
- ◆ Fast write (in which students write continuously on whatever comes to their mind when they reflect on a topic or idea): Social action.
- ◆ Share and reflect on responses.
- ◆ Introduce essential question.
- ◆ Initial written reflections on essential questions.
- ◆ Students share reflections.
- ◆ Exit question: What is something that stood out to you from our discussion today?

Key Standards Addressed:
- ◆ VA SOL 8.7: The student will write in a variety of forms to include narrative, expository, persuasive, and reflective with an emphasis on expository and persuasive writing.
- ◆ CCSS.ELA-LITERACY.W.8.4: Produce clear and coherent writing in which the development, organization, and style are appropriate to task, purpose, and audience.

Day Two: Introduction to Unit Texts

Key Learning Activities:
- ◆ Preview and introduce key themes in *The Epic Fail of Arturo Zamora*.
- ◆ Shared reading/listening: "My Shot" from *Hamilton*.
- ◆ Students share connections between the song and the question "What inspires individuals to take part in social action?"

- ◆ Introduce the unit's focal texts.
- ◆ Exit question: What is a text you've encountered that you think connects in some way to social action?

Key Standards Addressed:
- ◆ VA SOL 8.5: The student will read and analyze a variety of fictional texts, literary nonfiction, poetry, and drama.
- ◆ CCSS.ELA-LITERACY.RL.8.1: Cite the textual evidence that most strongly supports an analysis of what the text says explicitly as well as inferences drawn from the text.

Day Three: The Importance of Community

Before Class:
- ◆ Read Chapter One of *The Epic Fail of Arturo Zamora*.

Key Learning Activities:
- ◆ Fast write: "Community"
- ◆ Discussion: What role does community play in Chapter One of *The Epic Fail*?
- ◆ Response and discussion: To what communities does Arturo belong? How can those communities shape his actions and values?
- ◆ Shared reading/listening: "Keep Ya Head Up" by 2Pac.
- ◆ Expert-group responses: How does the concept of community connect to this song? What can we tell from this song about what 2Pac values? How does this song connect to the unit's essential question?
- ◆ Introduce final unit assessment.
- ◆ Exit question: Based on what we know so far about Arturo, what do you think could inspire him to take part in social action? How can you tell?

Key Standards Addressed:
- ◆ VA SOL 8.5: The student will read and analyze a variety of fictional texts, literary nonfiction, poetry, and drama.
- ◆ CCSS.ELA-LITERACY.RL.8.1: Cite the textual evidence that most strongly supports an analysis of what the text says explicitly as well as inferences drawn from the text.

Day Four: Who Brings Communities Together and Why?

Before Class:
- Read Chapters Two and Three of *The Epic Fail of Arturo Zamora*.

Key Learning Activities:
- Response: Describe someone who brings unity. Make a text to self, text to text, or text to world connection.
- Discussion: What inferences can we make about Abuela and her role in the community? What evidence supports these inferences?
- Written reflection and discussion: How can Abuela's presence in the community inspire social action?
- Shared reading: "I Have A White Rose to Tend" by José Martí.
- Small-group responses: How the "White Rose" helps create a community.
- Exit question: Return to the person you wrote about in our initial response. Connect that person to one of the two texts we discussed today.

Key Standards Addressed:
- VA SOL 8.5: The student will read and analyze a variety of fictional texts, literary nonfiction, poetry, and drama.
- CCSS.ELA-LITERACY.RL.8.1: Cite the textual evidence that most strongly supports an analysis of what the text says explicitly as well as inferences drawn from the text.
- CCSS.ELA-LITERACY.RL.8.2: Determine a theme or central idea of a text and analyze its development over the course of the text, including its relationship to the characters, setting, and plot; provide an objective summary of the text.

Day Five: Choosing to Take Social Action

Before Class:
- Read Chapters Four and Five of *The Epic Fail of Arturo Zamora*.

Key Learning Activities:
- Fast write: Creating change.
- Follow-up discussion: What challenges come with change?
- Shared listening: "The General" by Dispatch.

- ◆ Written response: How does this song relate to our essential question?
- ◆ Double-entry response: pages 45–47 of *The Epic Fail*.
- ◆ Discussion: What inspires Carmen and Arturo to take social action? Why them instead of other characters?
- ◆ Evidence-based prediction: How do you think the rest of the family will react to Carmen and Arturo taking social action?
- ◆ Exit question: Compare some aspect of "The General" with *The Epic Fail of Arturo Zamora*.

Key Standards Addressed:
- ◆ VA SOL 8.5: The student will read and analyze a variety of fictional texts, literary nonfiction, poetry, and drama.
- ◆ VA SOL 8.7: The student will write in a variety of forms to include narrative, expository, persuasive, and reflective with an emphasis on expository and persuasive writing.
- ◆ CCSS.ELA-LITERACY.RL.8.2: Determine a theme or central idea of a text and analyze its development over the course of the text, including its relationship to the characters, setting, and plot; provide an objective summary of the text.
- ◆ CCSS.ELA-LITERACY.RL.8.3: Analyze how particular lines of dialogue or incidents in a story or drama propel the action, reveal aspects of a character, or provoke a decision.

Day Six: Moving from Ideas to Action

Before Class:
- ◆ Read Chapters Six and Seven of *The Epic Fail of Arturo Zamora*.

Key Learning Activities:
- ◆ Response: two lines from text: "A little hope never hurt anyone" (p. 54) and "Love and faith are most important" (p. 57).
- ◆ Share highlights from responses and identify common themes.
- ◆ Discussion: Arturo and Carmen attend Wilfredo Pipo's rally in disguise; what does this show us about social action?
- ◆ Shared viewing and response: *Flower Thrower* by Banksy.
- ◆ Written response and verbal share: How does *Flower Thrower* inform our thoughts about this unit's essential question?

- ◆ Discussion: How can we connect *Flower Thrower* to events, characters, and issues in *The Epic Fail of Arturo Zamora*?
- ◆ Exit question: Based on our discussion and the texts we examined today, what is the role of hope in social action?

Key Standards Addressed:
- ◆ VA SOL 8.5: The student will read and analyze a variety of fictional texts, literary nonfiction, poetry, and drama.
- ◆ CCSS.ELA-LITERACY.RL.8.1: Cite the textual evidence that most strongly supports an analysis of what the text says explicitly as well as inferences drawn from the text.
- ◆ CCSS.ELA-LITERACY.RL.8.2: Determine a theme or central idea of a text and analyze its development over the course of the text, including its relationship to the characters, setting, and plot; provide an objective summary of the text.

Day Seven: Social Action that Changes the Present

Before Class:
- ◆ Read Chapters Eight, Nine, and Ten of *The Epic Fail of Arturo Zamora*.

Key Learning Activities:
- ◆ Response: One of the letters Arturo receives from Abuelo contains the line "A young person has the power to do many great things" (p. 89). Write a reflection on this quotation and its relevance to our unit.
- ◆ Group response follow-up: In groups, choose another line from one of the letters Arturo receives from Abuelo. On a piece of chart paper, write the line and three reasons why it is relevant to our unit.
- ◆ Discussion: How does Abuelo's message of love relate to the idea of deciding to get involved in social action?
- ◆ Written response: Why is it important to Arturo to show Carmen that he won't give up?
- ◆ Shared reading: "Wage Peace" by Judyth Hill.
- ◆ Reflection: Identify a line from this poem; what do you think that line shows us about social action?
- ◆ Discussion: Comparison of "Wage Peace" and *Flower Thrower*.

◆ Exit question: How does the message of "Wage Peace" compare to the letters Arturo receives from Abuelo? What similarities and differences do you notice?

Key Standards Addressed:
◆ VA SOL 8.5: The student will read and analyze a variety of fictional texts, literary nonfiction, poetry, and drama.
◆ CCSS.ELA-LITERACY.RL.8.1: Cite the textual evidence that most strongly supports an analysis of what the text says explicitly as well as inferences drawn from the text.
◆ CCSS.ELA-LITERACY.RL.8.5: Compare and contrast the structure of two or more texts and analyze how the differing structure of each text contributes to its meaning and style.

Day Eight: Social Action and Raising Awareness

Before Class:
◆ Read Chapters Eleven and Twelve of *The Epic Fail of Arturo Zamora.*

Key Learning Activities:
◆ Response: Reflect on Carmen and Arturo's conversation on pages 97–98 about gentrification. What is the importance of that conversation?
◆ Small-group reflection and discussion: Identify a line from these chapters that shows Arturo's thoughts on taking action. What can you infer from that line?
◆ Written response: Arturo is trying to raise awareness of the need to take action against Pipo Place. What challenges is he facing? How do you think he will address them?
◆ Shared viewing: *For Some, It's Mt. Everest* by the American Disabilities Association.
◆ Reflection and discussion: How does this image raise awareness for social action?
◆ Continued discussion: What similarities exist between this image and Arturo's experience?

◆ Exit question: How did viewing and discussing *For Some, It's Mt. Everest* contribute to your understanding of our unit's essential question?

Key Standards Addressed:
◆ VA SOL 8.5: The student will read and analyze a variety of fictional texts, literary nonfiction, poetry, and drama.
◆ VA SOL 8.6: The student will read, comprehend, and analyze a variety of nonfiction texts.
◆ CCSS.ELA-LITERACY.RL.8.1: Cite the textual evidence that most strongly supports an analysis of what the text says explicitly as well as inferences drawn from the text.

Day Nine: Finding the Courage to Act

Before Class:
◆ Read Chapters Thirteen and Fourteen of *The Epic Fail of Arturo Zamora*.

Key Learning Activities:
◆ Response: Revisit the José Martí poem on pages 125–126. What do you think the line about singing the verses of his soul means to Arturo?
◆ Small-group responses: 1) Describe the lunch at Wilfredo Pipo's office. 2) What do you infer about Wilfredo's conduct at the lunch? 3) Discuss how the events of the lunch may have contributed to Cari's decision to call a family meeting.
◆ Written reflection: Return to Abuelo's letter on page 131. What do you think Abuelo's message about poetry means to Arturo? How can you tell?
◆ Shared reading/listening: Excerpt from "Hero" by Nas.
◆ Response: What message does Nas send about taking action for others? How can you connect that to events and characters in *The Epic Fail of Arturo Zamora*?
◆ Discussion: Return again to the José Martí poem on pages 125–126. How does it connect to the message of "Hero"?
◆ Exit question: How does the idea of courage relate to one of the texts we discussed today?

Key Standards Addressed:
- ◆ VA SOL 8.5: The student will read and analyze a variety of fictional texts, literary nonfiction, poetry, and drama.
- ◆ CCSS.ELA-LITERACY.RL.8.1: Cite the textual evidence that most strongly supports an analysis of what the text says explicitly as well as inferences drawn from the text.
- ◆ CCSS.ELA-LITERACY.RL.8.2: Determine a theme or central idea of a text and analyze its development over the course of the text, including its relationship to the characters, setting, and plot; provide an objective summary of the text.

Day Ten: Connecting Social Action to the Real World

Before Class:
- ◆ Read Chapters Fifteen and Sixteen of *The Epic Fail of Arturo Zamora*.

Key Learning Activities:
- ◆ Response and discussion: Identify something from today's reading that struck you as important. Why did it strike you as important?
- ◆ Reflection: Identify a passage that stood out to you. What did that passage show you about the character or event described in the passage?
- ◆ Discussion of protest sign "Family is Community—Community is Family." How does that sign connect to our essential question?
- ◆ Introduction of article "7 Times in History When Students Turned to Activism" by Maggie Astor and discussion of the related assignment to read the article and bring in an article of the student's choice that addresses a social issue.
- ◆ Sharing of example article: "Activists to Retailers: Shoppers Need to Know Who's Making the Clothes" by Sophia Lepore.
- ◆ Sharing of resources for students to use to find articles of their choosing.
- ◆ Exit question: What is something from the "Activists to Retailers" article that stood out to you?

Key Standards Addressed:

- ◆ VA SOL 8.5: The student will read and analyze a variety of fictional texts, literary nonfiction, poetry, and drama.
- ◆ VA SOL 8.6: The student will read, comprehend, and analyze a variety of nonfiction texts.
- ◆ CCSS.ELA-LITERACY.RL.8.1: Cite the textual evidence that most strongly supports an analysis of what the text says explicitly as well as inferences drawn from the text.
- ◆ CCSS.ELA-LITERACY.W.8.9: Draw evidence from literary or informational texts to support analysis, reflection, and research.

Day Eleven: Sharing Real-World Examples

Before Class:

- ◆ Read "7 Times in History When Students Turned to Activism" and an article of the student's choice related to social action.

Key Learning Activities:

- ◆ Written reflection: Identify an event described in "7 Times in History When Students Turned to Activism" that stands out to you. What strikes you about this event? How does it inform your thinking about our essential question? (You will turn these in for formative assessment.)
- ◆ Identify and share highlights of reflections.
- ◆ Roundtable shares: Individuals share highlights from the articles they brought in for today with table-group members.
- ◆ Written response and small-group share: Compare the information, ideas, and actions in the article you've read for today with what we've read in *The Epic Fail of Arturo Zamora*.
- ◆ Volunteers share highlights with the whole class.
- ◆ Exit question: How did reading and discussing nonfiction examples of social action inform your thinking about this topic?

Key Standards Addressed:
- ◆ VA SOL 8.6: The student will read, comprehend, and analyze a variety of nonfiction texts.
- ◆ VA SOL 8.7: The student will write in a variety of forms to include narrative, expository, persuasive, and reflective with an emphasis on expository and persuasive writing.
- ◆ CCSS.ELA-LITERACY.RL.8.1: Cite the textual evidence that most strongly supports an analysis of what the text says explicitly as well as inferences drawn from the text.
- ◆ CCSS.ELA-LITERACY.W.8.9: Draw evidence from literary or informational texts to support analysis, reflection, and research.

Day Twelve: Facing Adversity

Before Class:
- ◆ Read Chapters Seventeen, Eighteen, and Nineteen of *The Epic Fail of Arturo Zamora*.

Key Learning Activities:
- ◆ Opening reflection: Revisit the section on pages 164 and 165 where Arturo describes his experience in writing. Why do you think Arturo spent so much time writing this information?
- ◆ Small-group response: Describe a challenge Arturo has faced in this book and either how he has faced the challenge or how you think he will face the challenge as the book continues.
- ◆ Shared reading: "Still I Rise" by Maya Angelou.
- ◆ Initial response: Identify an excerpt from this poem that strikes you and write why.
- ◆ Discussion: What message do you take from this poem?
- ◆ Written response and discussion: How can you connect the ideas in this poem with Arturo's experience?
- ◆ Exit question: How does "Still I Rise" contribute to the conversation about our essential question?

Key Standards Addressed:
- ◆ VA SOL 8.5: The student will read and analyze a variety of fictional texts, literary nonfiction, poetry, and drama.
- ◆ CCSS.ELA-LITERACY.RL.8.1: Cite the textual evidence that most strongly supports an analysis of what the text says explicitly as well as inferences drawn from the text.
- ◆ CCSS.ELA-LITERACY.RL.8.2: Determine a theme or central idea of a text and analyze its development over the course of the text, including its relationship to the characters, setting, and plot; provide an objective summary of the text.

Day Thirteen: Connections Between Memories and Actions

Before Class:
- ◆ Read Chapters Twenty, Twenty-One, and Twenty-Two of *The Epic Fail of Arturo Zamora*.

Key Learning Activities:
- ◆ Fast write: Remembering those important to us.
- ◆ Jigsaw groups: Class divides into three groups. Each group focuses on one chapter, answering this question: How does this chapter relate to Abuela's memory?
- ◆ Written response and discussion: What is the role of Abuela's death in this text?
- ◆ Evidence-based predictions: What do you think Arturo and his family will do next? What evidence supports these statements?
- ◆ Shared viewing and discussion: *Face 2 Face Project* by JR and Marco.
- ◆ Response: What might the artists have been trying to achieve by showing these photographs of Israelis and Palestinians? How is this an act of social action?
- ◆ Connection: The *Face 2 Face Project* addresses ideas of unity and overcoming differences. Do you see these themes in the description of Arturo and his family?
- ◆ Exit question: Choose either the reading we did for today or the *Face 2 Face Project* and comment on how it connects to our unit's essential question.

Key Standards Addressed:
- ◆ VA SOL 8.5: The student will read and analyze a variety of fictional texts, literary nonfiction, poetry, and drama.
- ◆ CCSS.ELA-LITERACY.RL.8.1: Cite the textual evidence that most strongly supports an analysis of what the text says explicitly as well as inferences drawn from the text.
- ◆ CCSS.ELA-LITERACY.RL.8.2: Determine a theme or central idea of a text and analyze its development over the course of the text, including its relationship to the characters, setting, and plot; provide an objective summary of the text.

Day Fourteen: Furthering Social Action

Before Class:
- ◆ Read Chapters Twenty-Three and Twenty-Four of *The Epic Fail of Arturo Zamora*.

Key Learning Activities:
- ◆ Opening response: Chapter Twenty-Three is called "Cooking From Memory." How does Arturo's cooking in this chapter relate to his memories of Abuela?
- ◆ Written response and discussion: Even though these chapters are about different topics (one is about Abuela's memorial and the other is about the city council's vote), they have some key similarities. What are some ways these chapters are related? How do they both connect to our essential question?
- ◆ Group activity: Each group takes one of the four songs or song excerpts we've discussed in this unit ("My Shot," "The General," "Keep Ya Head Up," and "Hero") and relates it to the characters and events we've read about so far in *The Epic Fail of Arturo Zamora*. Groups give informal presentations on their insights.
- ◆ Exit question: What is something in another group's presentation that you felt was especially strong?

Key Standards Addressed:
- ◆ VA SOL 8.5: The student will read and analyze a variety of fictional texts, literary nonfiction, poetry, and drama.
- ◆ CCSS.ELA-LITERACY.RL.8.1: Cite the textual evidence that most strongly supports an analysis of what the text says explicitly as well as inferences drawn from the text.
- ◆ CCSS.ELA-LITERACY.RL.8.2: Determine a theme or central idea of a text and analyze its development over the course of the text, including its relationship to the characters, setting, and plot; provide an objective summary of the text.

Day Fifteen: The Many Forms of Social Action

Before Class:
- ◆ Read Chapters Twenty-Five and Twenty-Six of *The Epic Fail of Arturo Zamora*, as well as the Epilogue.

Key Learning Activities:
- ◆ Response: At the end of page 231, Arturo says "Change *had* come. But I wasn't worried anymore." What kind of change do you think he is talking about? Why wasn't he worried?
- ◆ Reflection and discussion: Why do you think Arturo shared a poem at the meeting? What significance does this poem have?
- ◆ Group activity: Each group takes one of the three poems we've discussed in this unit ("I Have a White Rose to Tend," "Still I Rise," and "Wage Peace") and relates to the characters and events in *The Epic Fail of Arturo Zamora*. Groups give informal presentations on their insights.
- ◆ Class discussion: How do these poems resemble the poem Arturo shares on pages 224–225?
- ◆ Reflection and discussion: What do the events of the epilogue show us about social action?
- ◆ Conversation: What are some benefits that come from examining a wide range of texts like the ones in this unit? How does this compare to what you've done in other classes?
- ◆ Exit question: What is something you learned in this unit about what inspires individuals to take part in social action?

Key Standards Addressed:
- ◆ VA SOL 8.5: The student will read and analyze a variety of fictional texts, literary nonfiction, poetry, and drama.
- ◆ CCSS.ELA-LITERACY.RL.8.1: Cite the textual evidence that most strongly supports an analysis of what the text says explicitly as well as inferences drawn from the text.
- ◆ CCSS.ELA-LITERACY.RL.8.2: Determine a theme or central idea of a text and analyze its development over the course of the text, including its relationship to the characters, setting, and plot; provide an objective summary of the text.

Day Sixteen: Final Assessment Work Session

Before Class:
- ◆ Work on final unit assessment. Bring all drafts, outlines, ideas, and materials to class.

Key Learning Activities:
- ◆ Review of guidelines and rubric for final unit assessment.
- ◆ In-class work time on assessment.
- ◆ One-on-one conferences with teacher.
- ◆ Opportunities for peer feedback.
- ◆ Exit question: Describe the progress you made today on your assessment.

Key Standards Addressed:
- ◆ VA SOL 8.7: The student will write in a variety of forms to include narrative, expository, persuasive, and reflective with an emphasis on expository and persuasive writing.
- ◆ CCSS.ELA-LITERACY.W.8.1.B: Support claim(s) with logical reasoning and relevant evidence, using accurate, credible sources and demonstrating an understanding of the topic or text.
- ◆ CCSS.ELA-LITERACY.W.8.4: Produce clear and coherent writing in which the development, organization, and style are appropriate to task, purpose, and audience.
- ◆ CCSS.ELA-LITERACY.W.8.9: Draw evidence from literary or informational texts to support analysis, reflection, and research.

A note about this class meeting: If you want more time to confer with students, feel like they could benefit from extra in-class work time, or both, you may want to repeat this session to ensure students have the amount of support and time they need to successfully complete their assessments.

Day Seventeen: Final Assessment Publishing Celebration

Before Class:
◆ Complete final unit assessment. Bring a hard copy of your assessment for our publishing celebration and to turn in.

Key Learning Activities:
◆ Students share verbal summaries of the insights they shared in their assessments and the texts they selected.
◆ Assessment publishing celebration, in which students read one another's works and write positive comments on an attached sheet at the end of the piece.
◆ Exit question: What is something you read in a peer's assessment that impressed you?

Key Standards Addressed:
◆ VA SOL 8.7: The student will write in a variety of forms to include narrative, expository, persuasive, and reflective with an emphasis on expository and persuasive writing.
◆ CCSS.ELA-LITERACY.W.8.1.B: Support claim(s) with logical reasoning and relevant evidence, using accurate, credible sources and demonstrating an understanding of the topic or text.
◆ CCSS.ELA-LITERACY.W.8.4: Produce clear and coherent writing in which the development, organization, and style are appropriate to task, purpose, and audience.
◆ CCSS.ELA-LITERACY.W.8.9: Draw evidence from literary or informational texts to support analysis, reflection, and research.

Key Takeaway Ideas

◆ The purpose of this chapter is to illustrate one form an inquiry-oriented unit can take: in this case, a unit that features one whole-class text and a variety of additional works from a variety of disciplines and time periods that help students think about and ultimately respond to the unit's essential question.

◆ The unit described in this chapter is intended to provide one model for how such a unit can look. While you can certainly teach this unit to your students in its current form, we also suggest that, as you read the details of this unit, you think about how you might construct a unit that engages your students based on their interests and experiences. Our goal in describing this unit is to share an example that you can adapt to best align with the needs and interests of your students.

Suggestions for Creating Your Own Unit

◆ To start this process, reflect on one or more key essential questions that might especially engage your students. The essential question that guided the unit discussed in this chapter is a model of such a question. To do this, we recommend starting by simply listening to your students. You can make note of the interests and curiosities they bring up in class discussions and everyday conversations. For instance, Sean selected this unit's essential question because his students expressed a great deal of interest in social action.

◆ Another useful tactic is to ask students to complete interest inventory questionnaires that ask them to share topics and ideas about which they wonder or would like to investigate more thoroughly. These responses can then form essential questions that will guide inquiry-based units.

◆ After you've identified that question or those questions, we recommend identifying a central novel that you believe would engage and challenge your students while helping them reflect on the essential question or questions. To do this, we suggest considering the topics and issues that are central to this question and then reflecting on potential texts that address these issues and are aligned with your students' interests and grade level.

◆ For example, when selecting *The Epic Fail of Arturo Zamora* as the central text for the unit described in this chapter, Sean looked for a text that addressed the unit's essential question in both specific and generalizable ways: in this book, Arturo engages in social action that is local to a particular context, but can also be connected to other examples of social action and to insights about the topic in general. Similarly, we recommend selecting a text that address your unit's focus and essential question in both concrete ways and big-picture ones.

◆ Once you've thought about this novel, you can begin to think of additional texts that can work in concert with the novel to help your students consider the essential question(s) in nuanced and informed ways. We recommend incorporating a variety of genres and time periods in these texts to create an in-depth inquiry experience for your students.

Resources and Reminders

◆ Before teaching this unit to your students, we recommend creating a unit rationale that you'll share with administrators, parents, and students. Since inquiry-based learning is unfamiliar to some, this rationale can help you address and answer many of the questions you might be asked regarding the features and benefits of this type of unit. Like the example rationale in this chapter, we recommend creating a rationale that addresses the unit's focus, its key attributes, its connection to educational objectives (including state and national standards), and the unit's relevance to students' academic and societal needs. This rationale will show all interested parties that you have thought carefully about the benefits of this method of instruction and that you are implementing it with students' best interests in mind.

◆ Before you begin teaching the unit, decide on the summative assessment you'll ask students to complete at the unit's completion. We recommend aligning the assessment with the unit's essential question to ensure that the unit's assessment and instruction are closely aligned. In addition, we encourage you to create an assessment that allows for student choice by giving flexibility in the texts and resources they use when completing the assignment. For example, the assessment Sean used with his students required them to use the whole class novel, but also provided flexibility in the other resources that students used.

A Final Insight

◆ Teaching inquiry-based and multi-textual units like the one described in this chapter can be a lot of fun! Talk with your students about the intellectual enjoyment and challenge of approaching a complex essential question from a variety of perspectives and encourage them to immerse themselves in this complex and engaging work!

4

Student-Selected Text Sets
in an Inquiry-Driven Unit

In this chapter, we'll examine the second of the three inquiry-based units described in this section of the book. While some aspects of this unit are similar to the one discussed in Chapter Three, there are also significant differences; by reflecting on these similarities and differences and comparing these units, we'll consider the range of instructional possibilities created by inquiry-based literature instruction. Like the unit described in Chapter Three, Sean taught this unit to an eighth-grade English class—the same class to which he taught the previous unit. Also similar to the unit described in the previous chapter, the unit discussed here in Chapter Four asked students to reflect on and make a variety of connections to a thought-provoking, high-interest essential question—in this case, the essential question at the heart of the unit was "How and why do people challenge social norms?"

A key difference between this unit and the one described in Chapter Three is the way their respective texts were organized: while Chapter Three's unit had a class-wide text and an assigned text set, the unit described here represents a different construction that allows for increased student choice. In this unit, Sean read aloud the book *Bronx Masquerade* by Nikki Grimes, using this text as a starting point and a touchstone for the class's discussion of the essential question. In addition, students selected independent reading books that they felt aligned with that question; while reading these books, the students reflected on how the information in the texts helped them respond to the unit's focal question. Students selected these books from the classroom library, the school library, or another source they chose to access outside of school. Along with these independent reading books, students selected additional texts that they felt were connected to the essential question; specifically, students were asked to select two other texts (each representing a different genre, such as songs, poems, short stories, visual art, film, nonfiction articles, or other texts) that they felt addressed the essential question. When selecting their independent reading books and the other texts in the unit, students first reflected in class on the unit's essential question and possible texts that aligned with it. After that, they each created potential text set lists and annotations that they brought to class to discuss with Sean. In these documents, students listed the book they were considering for independent reading and the two other texts from different genres. In addition, they wrote brief annotations describing the texts and discussing each text in the context of the unit's essential question. By creating these documents, students were required to think carefully about the relationship between the texts they selected and the essential question.

The goal of this chapter is to describe a form of inquiry-based literature instruction that merges the strengths of inquiry-oriented and essential-question-driven learning with the benefits of independent reading and student choice. Doing so, we feel, incorporates the same positive instructional features of the inquiry-based unit described in Chapter Three while giving students the opportunity to make more decisions in the texts they read. The increased student choice in this unit is an example of the gradual release of responsibility (Pearson & Gallagher, 1983): once students have engaged in inquiry-based literacy instruction with a whole-class assigned text, they can take on more freedom to choose while still operating in a supportive and structured instructional context. Both of these unit forms have significant strengths; we encourage you to use both types to give your students a wide range of instructional experiences with inquiry-based learning.

We'll begin our examination of this unit by first considering its essential question: we'll explore that question by noting its academic significance, its relevance to students' lives, and the ways it can facilitate meaningful inquiry. After that, we'll reflect on the unit's read-aloud text, *Bronx Masquerade*, paying attention to how this text aligns with the unit's essential question and how it facilitated the students' independent text selections. Then, we'll examine the rationale that Sean shared with administrators, students, and families before teaching this unit to eighth-graders. Following that, we'll look together at the assessment Sean asked his students to complete at the conclusion of the unit. Next, we'll see outlines of the daily lesson plans used in the unit. Finally, we'll consider key takeaway ideas that you can connect to your own instruction.

As you read this chapter, we encourage you to think about how to engage your students in inquiry-based instruction that combines structure and freedom like the practices Sean used with his students. These students listened to, followed along with, and reflected on a read-aloud text related to the unit's essential question and then selected independent reading books and texts of other genres that they connected to the essential question. Once you finish this chapter, you'll have a strong understanding of the features of such a unit and will be well-positioned to conduct this type of instruction with your students. By examining the examples described here, you'll know what inquiry-oriented and wide-ranging essential questions look like, as well as corresponding read-aloud texts and instructional activities that incorporate texts of students' choice. While you read about the unit Sean conducted with his students, we encourage you to think about possible essential questions and associated read-aloud texts that you believe will resonate with and foster deep learning in your students. Now, let's begin our exploration of this exciting unit format by considering the essential question that Sean used with his students and the ideas related to it.

Essential Question

The essential question "How and why do people challenge social norms?" was especially well-suited for this unit's unique features. Since the unit called for students to reflect on a whole-class read-aloud text while also selecting their own independent-reading books and accompanying texts, Sean felt that the best essential question would be both specific and broad. He wanted an inquiry-oriented question specific enough to apply to the read-aloud text, but still broad enough to enable students to consider a wide variety of works for their self-selected text sets. This unit's question of how and why people challenge social norms met these criteria, as it can be applied to specific situations in which individuals go against social norms as well as broader discussions about why people make the decisions they do.

In addition to these important attributes, Sean felt that this essential question was a strong choice for his students because of its relevance to their lives. In class discussions, written work, and unstructured time, many students brought up the idea of societal expectations of individuals, commenting on how important it is for people to think critically about those expectations and defy them when those expectations did not align with their own beliefs and ideals. Students brought up this topic when talking about historical events, present-day scenarios, literary texts, and instances in their own lives. For example, Sean and other teachers at the school frequently heard students talk about the social norms and expectations they felt existed for young people their age, commenting on gender roles, stereotypes of individuals involved in athletic and artistic endeavors, and how they felt society expected them to pursue certain careers or possess specific interests for various reasons. In addition to demonstrating awareness of these social norms, students also voiced that they believed these societal expectations were problematic and wanted to challenge them. Given the students' keen interest in and awareness of this topic, Sean chose an essential question that was relevant to their concerns and provided opportunities for authentic inquiry.

Like the unit described in Chapter Three, the inquiry-based orientation of this unit and the wide range of texts to which it lent itself helped Sean align the unit with important instructional standards that call for students to read a wide range of texts and engage in the deep thinking associated with inquiry and essential questions. While specific state standards vary, inquiry-based literature units like this one achieve many essential learning goals that are valued in a range of contexts. When teaching this unit to his students, Sean identified alignment with the Common Core State Standards and the standards specific to Virginia, where this unit was taught. We encourage you to look at the standards specific to your context for learning goals that address students reading texts from a wide range of genres and engaging in the thoughtful analytical work with which inquiry is aligned. The thought-provoking and wide-ranging nature of this unit's essential question helped create a learning experience for students that allowed them to achieve these important academic benefits. Now that we've explored the benefits associated with this essential question, let's consider the features of the unit's read-aloud text.

The Unit's Read-Aloud Text

In this unit, the class shared a common experience through the read-aloud text *Bronx Masquerade* by Nikki Grimes. Told from the points of view of 18 students in a high-school English class, this novel contains short reflections and corresponding poems describing their authentic selves. Sean chose this text to occupy a central role in this unit because of its variety of perspectives and its alignment with the unit's essential question: the characters in this book represent a wide range of backgrounds, interests, and experiences, but a common theme in their reflections and poems is that there is more to them than society assumes. While expressing their true identities, students challenge those social norms that suggest they act in certain ways without regard for who they truly are. For example, one of the novel's students, Devon Hope, a basketball player who also loves poetry, expresses a desire to break free from expectations that he should hide his academic interests and only display his athletic skills: "Forget who I really am, who I really want to be. The law is be cool, be tough, play ball, and use books for weight training—not reading" (p. 29). Devon rejects the "law" he identifies and displays his interest in reading poetry, providing one of many excellent examples of ways in which characters in the book challenge social norms.

When Sean first introduced this book to his students, he explained that it aligned well with the unit's focus because of its wide-ranging depiction of how and why people challenge social norms. "There are definitely a lot of ways people challenge social norms," he told his students, "and that's going to make our unit really interesting. The book *Bronx Masquerade* that we'll use as our read-aloud text has a lot of different examples of people going against social norms." Later in that day's discussion, Sean added, "You're also going to pick your own independent reading books and other texts of different genres that show people going against social norms. While you think about these texts, I'll ask you to make connections to the examples we find in *Bronx Masquerade*."

As this excerpt from Sean's instruction conveys, one of the reasons *Bronx Masquerade* worked well as a read-aloud text for this unit is that it provided a touchstone for students to think about and reflect back on as they selected their own text sets related to the topic of how and why individuals challenge social norms. Since *Bronx Masquerade* addresses examples of social-norm defiance that have the potential to be relevant to students and contains a variety of perspectives, Sean felt it provided an accessible example of a book that connects to the unit's essential question. Once students had been introduced to that example, they could begin to think about independent reading books and texts from other genres that they felt aligned with the unit's focus. (Note: While Sean read *Bronx Masquerade* aloud to the students, the students also had individual copies they used to follow along and reflect on key ideas and characters. This helped the students when reflecting on this book for the final assessment, described later in this chapter.)

When you conduct this type of unit with your students, we encourage you to apply similar decision-making criteria to your selection of a read-aloud text. A strong read-aloud text for this purpose aligns with the unit's essential question, relates to students' interests, and connects to the unit's inquiry topic in a big-picture way that allows students to see it as a touchstone text as they identify their own independent reading books and texts from other genres and as they do analyses related to the unit's essential question. Sean considered all of these factors when selecting *Bronx Masquerade* as the read-aloud text for this unit. Now that we've explored key aspects of a strong read-aloud text, we'll look in the next section at the unit rationale that Sean created to describe the important features of this unit.

Rationale

This is the rationale that Sean shared with administrators, students, and families before he taught this unit in order to give everyone involved a complete understanding of the key attributes and benefits of this unit. We believe that an effective rationale is a great way to clearly convey important features and positive aspects of an instructional approach—especially one that may be new to some. By sharing a description of upcoming instructional practices, we teachers can create strong lines of communication with students' families, school administrators, and with our students themselves. Because of this, we encourage you to use this rationale as a model for one that you'll create to share with interested parties when you teach units like this one to your students. We describe some suggestions about unit rationales to consider in the "Key Takeaway Ideas" section at the end of this chapter.

This document describes the unit that Sean Ruday will be working on with his eighth-grade English class. It provides a rationale for the unit by identifying and describing four of its key aspects: 1) the unit's focus, 2) the unit's key attributes, 3) the unit's connection to educational objectives, and 4) the unit's relevance to students' needs. By reading this document, you'll gain an understanding of the unit's most important features and strengths.

The Unit's Focus

This work students do in this unit will be focused on the essential question "How and why do people challenge social norms?" Through a range of learning activities, students will think carefully and analytically about this question, using a novel that Sean will read aloud to the class, books that students individually choose to read on their own, and other texts of different genres that students select to inform their analyses. In addition, students will do a great deal of discussion during this unit; these conversations will be done in whole-class and small-group formats and will be opportunities for students to reflect on the essential question and how the texts they'll read contribute to their understandings. The goal of the unit is for students to use the class read-aloud text and a range of other texts of their choosing to reach nuanced and well-developed understandings related to the essential question.

The Unit's Key Attributes

Two key aspects of this unit that are designed to help students reflect on the essential question are the texts with which students will engage throughout the unit and the assessment that students will complete at the unit's conclusion. While there are other important components of the unit, such as whole-class and small-group discussions in which students will participate and informal written reflections designed to help students reflect on what they're learning, this section focuses on the unit's text and its final assessment.

In this unit, there will be one whole-class text: the novel *Bronx Masquerade* by Nikki Grimes. Sean will read this book aloud to the class, beginning each class meeting by reading a section of the book and leading the students in a conversation about key aspects of the text and how those aspects relate to the unit's essential question. (Students will have copies with which they will follow along.) In addition, students will select other texts connected to the essential question to read during the unit:

◆ An independent-reading book. Students will select an independent-reading fiction or nonfiction book that relates in some way to the essential question "How and why do people challenge social norms?" Students will reflect throughout the unit on ways their independent reading books align with key concepts in the unit.

◆ Two other texts from different genres. Students will select two additional texts, each representing a different genre from the other works examined as part of the unit. For example, students can select songs, poems, short stories, visual art, film, nonfiction articles, or other texts that they feel connect to the essential question. Just as they'll do with their independent-reading books, students will share written reflections throughout the unit on how these texts align with important ideas and topics in the unit.

The range of texts created through the combination of *Bronx Masquerade*, students' independent-reading selections, and their choices of texts from other genres will ensure the combination of structure and freedom. The unit's features will give students flexibility and agency while still requiring them to think carefully about the essential question and the ways the texts they select relate to that question.

The assessment that students will complete at the end of this unit asks them to write a reflective essay that uses all four of the texts they analyzed during the unit to respond to the essential question "How and why do people challenge social norms?" In this essay, students will synthesize the texts they've worked with during the unit to form a conclusion about what individuals do to challenge social norms and why they make the choices they do. While the specific texts students analyze will certainly depict different ways of challenging social norms, this assignment will challenge students to look deeper and identify common themes that exist in the specific ways characters and/or aspects of those texts challenge those norms and the ways and reasons they do so. By reaching these conclusions, students will be able to benefit from the deep learning aligned with inquiry-based instruction. The recommended length of this reflective essay is three to four pages.

The Unit's Connection to Educational Objectives

The innovative, inquiry-based, and multi-textual nature of this unit nicely connects with educational objectives that focus on students' abilities to interpret and synthesize ideas in a variety of texts across different genres. The variety of texts in the unit and the analytical work the students will do with those texts will prepare them for the higher-order thinking essential to the paired-passage text-dependent questions required by the most recent Virginia Standards of Learning for English, in which students analyze paired works of different genres that focus on similar topics.

[*Note to readers of this book: This unit, like the others described in this book, was taught in Virginia.*]

In addition, the unit's structure, assignments, and range of texts align closely with a number of important state and national standards for eighth-grade students. Some especially relevant Virginia Standards of Learning are:

- ◆ VA SOL 8.5: The student will read and analyze a variety of fictional texts, literary nonfiction, poetry, and drama.
- ◆ VA SOL 8.7: The student will write in a variety of forms to include narrative, expository, persuasive, and reflective with an emphasis on expository and persuasive writing.

(Virginia Department of Education, 2017)

On a national level, there are many Common Core State Standards that are closely aligned with the features of this unit, such as those listed below:

- ◆ CCSS.ELA-LITERACY.W.8.1.B: Support claim(s) with logical reasoning and relevant evidence, using accurate, credible sources and demonstrating an understanding of the topic or text.
- ◆ CCSS.ELA-LITERACY.W.8.4: Produce clear and coherent writing in which the development, organization, and style are appropriate to task, purpose, and audience.
- ◆ CCSS.ELA-LITERACY.W.8.9: Draw evidence from literary or informational texts to support analysis, reflection, and research.
- ◆ CCSS.ELA-LITERACY.RL.8.1: Cite the textual evidence that most strongly supports an analysis of what the text says explicitly as well as inferences drawn from the text.
- ◆ CCSS.ELA-LITERACY.RL.8.2: Determine a theme or central idea of a text and analyze its development over the course of the text,

including its relationship to the characters, setting, and plot; provide an objective summary of the text.

◆ CCSS.ELA-LITERACY.RL.8.3: Analyze how particular lines of dialogue or incidents in a story or drama propel the action, reveal aspects of a character, or provoke a decision.

(Common Core State Standards Initiative, 2010)

The many standards aligned with the instructional features of this unit convey the academic benefits associated with the inquiry-based and multi-textual components of this unit. By engaging in meaningful inquiry that centers on this unit's essential question and incorporates a variety of texts, students' learning experiences will connect to a number of important standards.

[*Note to readers of this book: A wonderful feature of inquiry-based learning is the way it easily connects to so many learning standards. As described in Chapter Three, the in-depth analysis facilitated by inquiry-based literature instruction aligns with educational objectives reflected in many sets of standards and learning goals. We encourage you to examine the specific standards in your state and identify ways those objectives align with the features of inquiry-based literature instruction, as Sean did in this rationale.*]

The Unit's Relevance to Students' Needs

Another important aspect of this unit is that it has significant relevance to students. This section describes three key ways in which this unit, which is driven by the essential question "How and why do people challenge social norms?", connects to students' academic and personal needs.

1. The unit can help students feel supported as they deal with social norms in their own lives.

   The topic of how and why individuals challenging social norms is something that is of high interest to many of our students—this school year, a number of students have identified instances when they feel society has expected them to act in ways that have been in opposition to their authentic selves. This unit can help students understand that they are not alone in feeling this way. It will convey to them that the disconnect between social norms and individuals' authentic identities is present in a variety of contexts. By reading about a range of situations in which individuals have challenged social norms in productive and positive ways, students will be able to consider constructive methods that can relate in various ways to their experiences. These models can help students feel supported as they consider social norms in their own lives and show them effective ways of challenging social norms that positively impact society as a whole by addressing problematic ideas and assumptions.

2. The unit can help students synthesize a wide range of texts.

    Since this unit asks for students to consider a variety of texts related to its essential question, it can improve their abilities to interpret and synthesize a range of works representing distinct perspectives and genres. The variety of texts with which students will engage—*Bronx Masquerade*, the independent reading book each student selects, and the two other works representing different genres—will give them experience drawing connections between and identifying differences in a cross-section of works. Students will engage in this synthesis-oriented work throughout the unit, starting with the selections of their individual texts and culminating in the final assessment that asks students to synthesize the texts they've worked with during the unit to form a conclusion about what individuals do to challenge social norms and why they make the choices they do.

3. The unit can help students think analytically about real-world situations.

    An especially beneficial aspect of this unit is that the analytical thinking students do throughout can be applied to the real world. As students think carefully about how and why individuals challenge social norms, they will gain understandings of the contexts and processes in which those events take place. Not only do the events and characters in *Bronx Masquerade* reflect a number of authentic, real-world instances in which people challenge social norms, but students will also have the opportunity to select texts that represent their out-of-school lives and experiences, such as songs, films, and nonfiction articles that address examples of individuals who challenge social norms. The focus and format of this unit facilitates connections to and analysis of real-world situations that align with its essential question.

Sean is very excited to work with the students on this unit! He feels it represents the best practices of English instruction and has the potential to benefit our students in a number of important ways. He is happy to talk further about it and encourages you to contact him at sean.ruday@gmail.com with any questions or comments.

Assessment

This section provides information about the assessment that Sean's students completed at the end of this unit. It contains the assessment description Sean distributed to his students and the rubric he used when evaluating students' works. As discussed in the assessment description, students were asked to write a reflective essay that used all four of the texts they analyzed during the unit to respond to the essential question "How and why do people challenge social norms?" Since this unit incorporated a great deal of student choice in the texts they read, that choice naturally extended to this assessment. When creating assessments for similar units you conduct with your students, we recommend asking students to synthesize the texts they examined in the unit in a response to the essential question. In addition, we suggest sharing the assessment description very early in the unit and providing your students with the evaluation criteria at that time. You can find additional assessment information in the "Key Takeaway Ideas" section later in this chapter and in Chapter Six, "Assessing Inquiry."

Assessment Description Distributed to Students

As you know, the essential question we're exploring in this unit is "How and why do people challenge social norms?" For the unit's assessment, you will write a reflective essay that answers the essential question and uses all four of the texts you analyzed during this unit to support your response. (Those four texts are *Bronx Masquerade*, your independent reading book, and the two other texts from different genres that you selected.) In this essay, you will synthesize these texts to form a conclusion about what individuals do to challenge social norms and why they make the choices they do. As you do this, ask yourself what common themes exist in the specific ways individuals in your texts challenge those norms and the reasons they do so.

You will need to cite these texts directly in your essay and describe how they inform your thinking regarding your response to our essential question. (You will also cite them in a Works Cited page following the reflection.) The recommended length of your reflection is three to four typed pages in Times New Roman, double-spaced, not including the Works Cited page. I will hold individual conferences with you as you write this piece. I am happy to answer any questions you have and am very excited to see what you create!

Assessment Rubric

"HOW AND WHY DO PEOPLE CHALLENGE SOCIAL NORMS?"

UNIT ASSESSMENT RUBRIC

Criteria	1	2	3	4	Feedback
Insights • Does the author's response provide thoughtful insights that address the unit's essential question "How and why do people challenge social norms?" • Are these insights clear, specific, and detailed? • Do the author's points convey a deep and nuanced understanding of how and why people challenge social norms?					
Textual support • Are the author's insights supported with specific and detailed connections to the specified texts (*Bronx Masquerade*, your independent reading book, and the two other texts from different genres that you selected)? • Does the author effectively communicate the relationship between these texts and the unit's essential question? • Is it clear that the author has carefully analyzed these texts with the unit's essential question in mind?					
Organization • Is the paper clearly organized? • Are paragraphs used in the paper's organization? • Is it clear when the author moves from one "train of thought" to another?					
Mechanics • Does the writing utilize proper mechanics? • Does it demonstrate an understanding of proper punctuation? • Are sentences clear and representative of complete thoughts? • Is capitalization used at appropriate times?					

1-criteria not met;   2-criteria partially met;   3-criteria met;   4-criteria exceeded

Total score:

Overall feedback:

Daily Lesson Plans

This section contains outlines of the daily lesson plans Sean used in this unit. Each day's description lists the day's focus, any work done before class, the main learning activities, and key state and national standards addressed in the day's lesson. These lesson plan outlines provide an example of how an inquiry-based unit that incorporates a whole-class read-aloud text and students' independent reading selections can look. We suggest using these plan outlines to inform your planning as you create similar units for your students!

Day One: Introduction of Essential Question

Key Learning Activities:
- ◆ Fast write (a low-stakes writing activity in which students write what comes to their mind when they think about a topic): Social norms.
- ◆ Share and reflect on responses.
- ◆ Follow-up fast write: Challenging social norms.
- ◆ Introduce essential question.
- ◆ Initial written reflections on essential question.
- ◆ Students share reflections.
- ◆ Exit question: Why do you think it's important to think about the idea of challenging social norms?

Key Standards Addressed:
- ◆ VA SOL 8.7: The student will write in a variety of forms to include narrative, expository, persuasive, and reflective with an emphasis on expository and persuasive writing.
- ◆ CCSS.ELA-LITERACY.W.8.4: Produce clear and coherent writing in which the development, organization, and style are appropriate to task, purpose, and audience.

Day Two: Introduction to Unit Features

Key Learning Activities:
- ◆ Preview and introduce key themes in *Bronx Masquerade*.
- ◆ Read aloud from *Bronx Masquerade*: "Wesley 'Bad Boy' Boone" pp. 3–6.
- ◆ Responses: What can you infer about Wesley from his description of Langston Hughes? How does Wesley challenge social norms?

- Discussion of the unit's text features and requirements.
- Students brainstorm potential texts.
- Exit question: What is a text you've encountered that addresses the concept of challenging social norms?

Key Standards Addressed:
- VA SOL 8.5: The student will read and analyze a variety of fictional texts, literary nonfiction, poetry, and drama.
- VA SOL 8.7: The student will write in a variety of forms to include narrative, expository, persuasive, and reflective with an emphasis on expository and persuasive writing.
- CCSS.ELA-LITERACY.RL.8.1: Cite the textual evidence that most strongly supports an analysis of what the text says explicitly as well as inferences drawn from the text.

Day Three: The Power of "Future"/Exploring Potential Texts

Before Class:
- Create a potential text-set list and annotation: List the book you would like to use for independent reading during the unit and the two other texts from different genres. For each text, write a brief annotation describing it and discussing how it connects to the essential question. Bring your proposed independent reading book to class.

Key Learning Activities:
- Fast write: "Future."
- Read aloud from *Bronx Masquerade:* "Tyrone Bittings" pp. 7–11.
- Responses: What is the importance of the future to Tyrone? Why do you think Tyrone ends his poem the way he does?
- Small-group responses: How does thinking about the future relate to challenging social norms?
- Partner discussion: Share your text-set ideas with your partner. Partners respond with insights. Teacher circulates.
- Teacher meets with students to discuss their text sets. Students begin reading independent reading book when text set is approved. Revision suggestions to text sets made as needed.

- ◆ Introduce final unit assessment.
- ◆ Exit question: How do you think challenging social norms in the present can impact the future?

Key Standards Addressed:
- ◆ VA SOL 8.5: The student will read and analyze a variety of fictional texts, literary nonfiction, poetry, and drama.
- ◆ VA SOL 8.7: The student will write in a variety of forms to include narrative, expository, persuasive, and reflective with an emphasis on expository and persuasive writing.
- ◆ CCSS.ELA-LITERACY.RL.8.1: Cite the textual evidence that most strongly supports an analysis of what the text says explicitly as well as inferences drawn from the text.

Day Four: Addressing Injustice

- ◆ Before class: Read independent reading book for 20 minutes. Bring book to class.

Key Learning Activities:
- ◆ Response: What is an example of injustice that you've witnessed?
- ◆ Read aloud from *Bronx Masquerade*: "Chankara Troupe" pp. 12–17.
- ◆ Responses: What can you infer about Chankara from the way she deals with Johnny's behavior? What impact does Chankara's poem have on Tyrone?
- ◆ Written reflection: How does the topic of injustice play a role in your independent reading book? How do characters react to it?
- ◆ Discussion: What do social norms and injustice have in common? (Students use background knowledge, independent reading books, and other works to inform their insights.)
- ◆ Reading workshop: Students read independent reading books and note connections to the day's discussion in their response journals.
- ◆ Share: Students share connections they noted.

- ◆ Exit question: What have you noticed so far about the social norms in your independent reading book and how they are challenged?

Key Standards Addressed:
- ◆ VA SOL 8.5: The student will read and analyze a variety of fictional texts, literary nonfiction, poetry, and drama.
- ◆ VA SOL 8.7: The student will write in a variety of forms to include narrative, expository, persuasive, and reflective with an emphasis on expository and persuasive writing.
- ◆ CCSS.ELA-LITERACY.RL.8.1: Cite the textual evidence that most strongly supports an analysis of what the text says explicitly as well as inferences drawn from the text.
- ◆ CCSS.ELA-LITERACY.RL.8.3: Analyze how particular lines of dialogue or incidents in a story or drama propel the action, reveal aspects of a character, or provoke a decision.

Day Five: Challenging Others' Assumptions

Before Class:
- ◆ Read independent reading book for 20 minutes. Bring book to class.
- ◆ Bring one of the texts from a different genre that you've selected to analyze.

Key Learning Activities:
- ◆ Reflection: What does it mean to challenge others' assumptions? What are some examples you can think of (from your life, a text, or another's life)?
- ◆ Read aloud from *Bronx Masquerade*: "Raul Ramirez" pp. 18–23.
- ◆ Responses: Why do you think Raul wants to paint the people he discusses doing the things he describes? What does Raul mean when he says, "you're more comfortable with myth than man" (p. 22)?
- ◆ Partner share: Discuss the different-genre text you brought to class with a partner. Share its main features and how it connects to the idea of challenging social norms.
- ◆ Whole-class share: Volunteers share main features of texts.
- ◆ Reflection: What assumptions or expectations are challenged in the text you selected?

- ◆ Small-group discussion: What assumptions or expectations exist for the main character in your independent reading book?
- ◆ Reading workshop: Students read independent reading books and note in their response journals how the main character deals with assumptions and expectations.
- ◆ Whole-class share: Students share connections they noted.
- ◆ Exit question: How does challenging others' assumptions and expectations relate to the unit's essential question of "How and why do people challenge social norms?"

Key Standards Addressed:
- ◆ VA SOL 8.5: The student will read and analyze a variety of fictional texts, literary nonfiction, poetry, and drama.
- ◆ VA SOL 8.7: The student will write in a variety of forms to include narrative, expository, persuasive, and reflective with an emphasis on expository and persuasive writing.
- ◆ CCSS.ELA-LITERACY.RL.8.2: Determine a theme or central idea of a text and analyze its development over the course of the text, including its relationship to the characters, setting, and plot; provide an objective summary of the text.
- ◆ CCSS.ELA-LITERACY.RL.8.3: Analyze how particular lines of dialogue or incidents in a story or drama propel the action, reveal aspects of a character, or provoke a decision.

Day Six: Expressing Authentic Selves

Before Class:
- ◆ Read independent reading book for 20 minutes. Bring book to class.
- ◆ Bring both of the texts from different genres that you selected to analyze.

Key Learning Activities:
- ◆ Fast write: "True self."
- ◆ Discussion: What stands in the way of individuals expressing their authentic selves?

◆ Read aloud from *Bronx Masquerade*: "Diondra Jordan" (pp. 24–28) and "Devon Hope" (pp. 29–33).

◆ Responses: What difficulties do Diondra and Devon face in expressing their authentic selves? What similarities and differences do you notice between these characters? Why do you think Devon's poem is called "Bronx Masquerade"?

◆ Discussion: How does the idea of expressing your authentic self connect to your life? Do you feel that things stand in the way of you expressing your authentic self? Why or why not?

◆ Reflection: Connect one of your different-genre texts to the idea of expressing one's true self.

◆ Partner share: Share highlights from your written reflection.

◆ Reading workshop: Students read their independent reading books and note in their responses journals connections to the idea of expressing one's true self. Are there obstacles that stand in the way of the way of individuals expressing their true selves?

◆ Whole-class share: Students share connections they made.

◆ Exit question: Based on our work in class today, how does the idea of expressing one's authentic self relate to our essential question of "How and why do people challenge social norms?"

Key Standards Addressed:

◆ VA SOL 8.5: The student will read and analyze a variety of fictional texts, literary nonfiction, poetry, and drama.

◆ VA SOL 8.7: The student will write in a variety of forms to include narrative, expository, persuasive, and reflective with an emphasis on expository and persuasive writing.

◆ CCSS.ELA-LITERACY.RL.8.1: Cite the textual evidence that most strongly supports an analysis of what the text says explicitly as well as inferences drawn from the text.

◆ CCSS.ELA-LITERACY.RL.8.2: Determine a theme or central idea of a text and analyze its development over the course of the text, including its relationship to the characters, setting, and plot; provide an objective summary of the text.

Day Seven: Rejecting Harmful Messages

Before Class:
- Read independent reading book for 20 minutes. Bring book to class.
- Bring both of the texts from different genres that you selected to analyze.

Key Learning Activities:
- Reflection: What are some messages in society that have the potential to be harmful?
- Volunteers share highlights from reflections.
- Read aloud from *Bronx Masquerade:* "Janelle Battle" (pp. 46–50).
- Responses: How do harmful messages impact Janelle? Why do you think Janelle says "I don't bruise easily" in her poem?
- Small-group discussion: What are some ways you've seen people reject harmful societal messages?
- Volunteers share with whole class.
- Reflection: Connect one of your different-genre texts to the idea of harmful messages. Does the piece address a potential harmful message? Does it reject the message?
- Partner share: Share highlights from your written reflection.
- Reading workshop: Students read their independent reading books and note in their response journals connections to the idea of harmful messages, responding to ideas such as "Is a potentially harmful message addressed and rejected in the book?"
- Whole-class share: Students share their responses.
- Exit question: How does the idea of rejecting harmful societal messages relate to our essential question of "How and why do people challenge social norms?"

Key Standards Addressed:
- VA SOL 8.5: The student will read and analyze a variety of fictional texts, literary nonfiction, poetry, and drama.
- VA SOL 8.7: The student will write in a variety of forms to include narrative, expository, persuasive, and reflective with an emphasis on expository and persuasive writing.

◆ CCSS.ELA-LITERACY.RL.8.2: Determine a theme or central idea of a text and analyze its development over the course of the text, including its relationship to the characters, setting, and plot; provide an objective summary of the text.
◆ CCSS.ELA-LITERACY.RL.8.3: Analyze how particular lines of dialogue or incidents in a story or drama propel the action, reveal aspects of a character, or provoke a decision.

Day Eight: The Importance of Support to Challenging Social Norms

Before Class:
◆ Read independent reading book for 20 minutes. Bring book to class.
◆ Bring both of the texts from different genres that you selected to analyze.

Key Learning Activities:
◆ Response: Think about a time you were supported in doing something difficult. What was the support like? What impact did it have?
◆ Volunteers share highlights of their responses.
◆ Read aloud from *Bronx Masquerade*: "Leslie Lucas" (pp. 51–56).
◆ Responses: What kind of support does Leslie receive from her classmates? How have Open Mike Fridays impacted Leslie? Why do you think Leslie says, "the scariest thing I can think of now is being all alone in the world" (p. 54)?
◆ Class discussion: Why do you think support is important when challenging social norms?
◆ Reflection: Reflect on the different-genre texts you brought to class today. How can you connect the idea of having the support of others to one or both of those texts? What supports do or do not exist? What role does having the support of others play in the text?
◆ Partner share: Share highlights from your written responses.
◆ Reading workshop: Students read their independent reading books and note in their response journals connections to the idea of support, identifying how the concept of support is or

is not present in the piece, noting examples of support, and reflecting on the impact of that support to the way a character in the book challenges social norms.
◆ Whole-class share: Students share their responses.
◆ Exit question: Identify one of the texts you considered today (*Bronx Masquerade*, one of your different-genre texts, or your independent reading book). In that text, how does support relate to the challenging of social norms?

Key Standards Addressed:
◆ VA SOL 8.5: The student will read and analyze a variety of fictional texts, literary nonfiction, poetry, and drama.
◆ VA SOL 8.7: The student will write in a variety of forms to include narrative, expository, persuasive, and reflective with an emphasis on expository and persuasive writing.
◆ CCSS.ELA-LITERACY.RL.8.1: Cite the textual evidence that most strongly supports an analysis of what the text says explicitly as well as inferences drawn from the text.
◆ CCSS.ELA-LITERACY.RL.8.2: Determine a theme or central idea of a text and analyze its development over the course of the text, including its relationship to the characters, setting, and plot; provide an objective summary of the text.

Day Nine: Challenging "Boxes"

Before Class:
◆ Read independent reading book for 20 minutes. Bring book to class.
◆ Bring both of the texts from different genres that you selected to analyze.

Key Learning Activities:
◆ Fast write: "Boxes."
◆ Volunteers share highlights from fast writes.
◆ Whole-class discussion: Have you ever felt like you were figuratively trapped in a box? Why do you think people sometimes feel like they're expected to act certain ways?
◆ Read aloud from *Bronx Masquerade*: "Tanisha Scott" (pp. 74–81) and "Devon" (pp. 82–85).

- Responses: Why does Tanisha appreciate Diondra and Janelle so much? What does Devon mean when he says, "I'm allergic to boxes" (p. 84)? What does Tyrone's statement about boxes show us about the book *Bronx Masquerade* as a whole?
- Whole-class discussion: How does rejecting the "boxes" Devon describes relate to our essential question of "How and why do people challenge social norms?"
- Reflection: Reflect on the different-genre texts you brought to class today. How can you connect the idea of being expected to act in a certain way (trapped in a figurative box) to one or both of those texts? Does anything in the text or texts reject the expectations (or "box") like characters in *Bronx Masquerade* did?
- Partner share: Share highlights from your written responses.
- Reading workshop: Students read their independent reading books and note in their response journals connections to the idea of being expected to act in a certain way (trapped in a figurative box). They will also reflect on any ways that characters in the text reject the expectations (or "boxes") like characters in *Bronx Masquerade* did?
- Whole-class share: Students share their responses.
- Exit question: Select one of the texts you reflected on today (*Bronx Masquerade*, one of your different-genre texts, or your independent reading book). Describe a way that the text discusses the idea of rejecting expectations to act in a certain way.

Key Standards Addressed:
- VA SOL 8.5: The student will read and analyze a variety of fictional texts, literary nonfiction, poetry, and drama.
- VA SOL 8.7: The student will write in a variety of forms to include narrative, expository, persuasive, and reflective with an emphasis on expository and persuasive writing.
- CCSS.ELA-LITERACY.RL.8.2: Determine a theme or central idea of a text and analyze its development over the course of the text, including its relationship to the characters, setting, and plot; provide an objective summary of the text.
- CCSS.ELA-LITERACY.RL.8.3: Analyze how particular lines of dialogue or incidents in a story or drama propel the action, reveal aspects of a character, or provoke a decision.

Day Ten: How Values Lead to Challenging Social Norms

Before Class:
- Read independent reading book for 20 minutes. Bring book to class.
- Bring both of the texts from different genres that you selected to analyze.

Key Learning Activities:
- Fast write: "Values."
- Volunteers share highlights from fast writes.
- Whole-class discussion: How does the concept of values relate to our unit essential question of "How and why do people challenge social norms?"
- Read aloud from *Bronx Masquerade:* "Sterling S. Hughes" (pp. 87–94).
- Responses: In what ways does Sterling feel like he challenges social norms? What can you infer about Sterling from his desire to become a teacher?
- Reflection: Reflect on the different genre texts you brought to class today. How does the content of one or both of those texts relate to the idea of one's values leading them to challenge social norms?
- Partner share: Share highlights from written responses.
- Volunteers share responses with whole class.
- Reading workshop: Students read their independent reading books and note in their response journals connections to the idea of one's values leading them to challenge social norms. They will note examples of this and compare them to the content in *Bronx Masquerade* and to the texts they examined in the previous activity.
- Whole-class discussion: Students share their responses and connections.
- Exit question: What did today's discussion and activities show you about the relationship between one's values and the essential question of "How and why do people challenge social norms?"

Key Standards Addressed:
- VA SOL 8.5: The student will read and analyze a variety of fictional texts, literary nonfiction, poetry, and drama.

- ◆ VA SOL 8.7: The student will write in a variety of forms to include narrative, expository, persuasive, and reflective with an emphasis on expository and persuasive writing.
- ◆ CCSS.ELA-LITERACY.RL.8.1: Cite the textual evidence that most strongly supports an analysis of what the text says explicitly as well as inferences drawn from the text.
- ◆ CCSS.ELA-LITERACY.W.8.9: Draw evidence from literary or informational texts to support analysis, reflection, and research.

Day Eleven: The Connection Between Ambition and Challenging Social Norms

Before Class:
- ◆ Read independent reading book for 20 minutes. Bring book to class.
- ◆ Bring both of the texts from different genres that you selected to analyze.

Key Learning Activities:
- ◆ Fast write: "Ambition."
- ◆ Volunteers share highlights from fast writes.
- ◆ Whole-class discussion: How do you think the idea of ambition can connect to challenging social norms?
- ◆ Read-aloud from *Bronx Masquerade:* "Steve Ericson" (pp. 114–122).
- ◆ Responses: What role does ambition play in Steve's life? What advice does Steve have about sharing one's dreams with others? Why do you think Steve says "Pack your dreams. They're portable" (p. 120)?
- ◆ Reflection: Reflect on the different-genre texts you brought to class today. What ambitions, goals, or dreams are expressed in one or both of those texts?
- ◆ Partner share: Share highlights from written responses.
- ◆ Volunteers share highlights with whole class.
- ◆ Partner share follow-up: How can you connect the ambitions, goals, or dreams you identified in your response to the idea of challenging social norms?

- ◆ Reading workshop: Students read their independent reading books and note in their response journals the ambitions, goals, or dreams expressed in the text. In addition, they see if they can connect the expressed ambitions, goals, or dreams to the idea of challenging social norms.
- ◆ Whole-class discussion: Students share their responses and connections.
- ◆ Exit question: Identify an example from today's class (from *Bronx Masquerade*, one of your different-genre texts, or your independent reading book) that describes an ambition and relates to the idea of challenging social norms. Why does this example relate to the idea of challenging social norms?

Key Standards Addressed:
- ◆ VA SOL 8.5: The student will read and analyze a variety of fictional texts, literary nonfiction, poetry, and drama.
- ◆ VA SOL 8.7: The student will write in a variety of forms to include narrative, expository, persuasive, and reflective with an emphasis on expository and persuasive writing.
- ◆ CCSS.ELA-LITERACY.RL.8.1: Cite the textual evidence that most strongly supports an analysis of what the text says explicitly as well as inferences drawn from the text.
- ◆ CCSS.ELA-LITERACY.RL.8.3: Analyze how particular lines of dialogue or incidents in a story or drama propel the action, reveal aspects of a character, or provoke a decision.

Day Twelve: Battling Inaccurate Perceptions

Before Class:
- ◆ Read independent reading book for 20 minutes. Bring book to class.
- ◆ Bring both of the texts from different genres that you selected to analyze.

Key Learning Activities:
- Opening reflection: What are some inaccurate perceptions you believe exist about young people?
- Volunteers share reflection highlights.
- Follow-up discussion: How can the inaccurate perceptions that exist about young people connect to our essential question "How and why do people challenge social norms?"
- Read aloud from *Bronx Masquerade:* "Tyrone" (pp. 128–129) and "News at Five" (pp. 130–132).
- Responses: What do the speakers in "News at Five" want us to understand about their true selves? What do you do think the line "News at Five has got you thinking I was born to steal" is meant to express to the reader? Why do you think the speakers in this poem discuss racial unity?
- Reflection: Reflect on the different-genre texts you brought to class today. How does the content of one or both texts relate to the idea of inaccurate perceptions?
- Partner share: Share highlights from written responses.
- Volunteers share highlights with whole class.
- Partner share follow-up: How do the ideas in your reflection relate to the idea of challenging social norms?
- Reading workshop: Students read their independent reading books and note in their response journals connections they can make to the idea of inaccurate perceptions. In addition, they reflect on how these connections can relate to the idea of challenging social norms.
- Whole-class discussion: Students share their responses.
- Exit question: What did today's discussion and activities show you about the relationship between inaccurate perceptions and the unit's essential question of "How and why do people challenge social norms?"

Key Standards Addressed:
- VA SOL 8.5: The student will read and analyze a variety of fictional texts, literary nonfiction, poetry, and drama.
- VA SOL 8.7: The student will write in a variety of forms to include narrative, expository, persuasive, and reflective with an emphasis on expository and persuasive writing.

◆ CCSS.ELA-LITERACY.RL.8.1: Cite the textual evidence that most strongly supports an analysis of what the text says explicitly as well as inferences drawn from the text.

◆ CCSS.ELA-LITERACY.W.8.9: Draw evidence from literary or informational texts to support analysis, reflection, and research.

Day Thirteen: The Freedom to Make Decisions

Before Class:

◆ Read independent reading book for 20 minutes. Bring book to class.

◆ Bring both of the texts from different genres that you selected to analyze.

Key Learning Activities:

◆ Response: Have you ever felt influenced to make a choice you didn't want to make?

◆ Volunteers share response highlights.

◆ Read aloud from *Bronx Masquerade:* "Diondra" (pp. 152–156).

◆ Response questions: Why do you think Diondra compares her father's choice to her drowning? What can you infer about Diondra from her narrative and poem?

◆ Follow-up discussion: At the end of today's read-aloud, Tyrone says "The future is ours. Let us have it." How does that statement relate to our essential question "How and why do people challenge social norms?"

◆ Reflection: Reflect on one or both of the different-genre texts you brought to class today. How does the idea of being able to make one's own decisions play a role in one or both of those texts?

◆ Partner share: Share highlights from written responses.

◆ Volunteers share highlights with whole class.

◆ Partner share follow-up: How does the information in your reflection about the freedom to make one's own decisions relate to the idea of challenging social norms?

◆ Reading workshop: Students read their independent reading books and note in their response journals connections they can make to the idea of being free to make one's own decisions, commenting on choices characters want to make and obstacles that stand in the way of them making those choices.

- Whole-class discussion: Students share their responses.
- Exit question: How did today's discussion and activities regarding being free to make one's own choices contribute to your understanding of our essential question "How and why do people challenge social norms?"

Key Standards Addressed:

- VA SOL 8.5: The student will read and analyze a variety of fictional texts, literary nonfiction, poetry, and drama.
- VA SOL 8.7: The student will write in a variety of forms to include narrative, expository, persuasive, and reflective with an emphasis on expository and persuasive writing.
- CCSS.ELA-LITERACY.RL.8.1: Cite the textual evidence that most strongly supports an analysis of what the text says explicitly as well as inferences drawn from the text.
- CCSS.ELA-LITERACY.RL.8.3: Analyze how particular lines of dialogue or incidents in a story or drama propel the action, reveal aspects of a character, or provoke a decision.

Day Fourteen: Changing Peoples' Minds

Before Class:

- Read independent reading book for 20 minutes. Bring book to class.
- Bring both of the texts from different genres that you selected to analyze.

Key Learning Activities:

- Fast write: "Changing peoples' minds."
- Read aloud from *Bronx Masquerade*: "Porscha Johnson" (pp. 157–161).
- Response: Why does Porscha want to change others' minds about her? Why do you think Porscha identifies ways her

classmates changed her mind about them? What do you think is the importance of Porscha writing "Mom, I finally forgive you" (p. 161)?

- ◆ Follow-up discussion: How do you think is the idea of changing peoples' minds related to our essential question "How and why do people challenge social norms?"
- ◆ Reflection: Reflect on one or both of the different-genre texts you brought to class today. How does the idea of changing peoples' minds play a role in one or both of those texts?
- ◆ Partner share: Share highlights from written responses.
- ◆ Volunteers share highlights with whole class.
- ◆ Partner share follow-up: How do the ideas you shared in your reflection relate to the idea of challenging social norms?
- ◆ Reading workshop: Students read their independent reading books and note in their response journals connections they can make to the idea of changing peoples' minds, noting how characters in their books change others' minds and what led them to do so.
- ◆ Whole-class discussion: Students share their responses.
- ◆ What did today's discussion and activities show you about the relationship between the idea of changing peoples' minds and our unit's essential question of "How and why do people challenge social norms?"

Key Standards Addressed:

- ◆ VA SOL 8.5: The student will read and analyze a variety of fictional texts, literary nonfiction, poetry, and drama.
- ◆ VA SOL 8.7: The student will write in a variety of forms to include narrative, expository, persuasive, and reflective with an emphasis on expository and persuasive writing.
- ◆ CCSS.ELA-LITERACY.RL.8.1: Cite the textual evidence that most strongly supports an analysis of what the text says explicitly as well as inferences drawn from the text.
- ◆ CCSS.ELA-LITERACY.RL.8.3: Analyze how particular lines of dialogue or incidents in a story or drama propel the action, reveal aspects of a character, or provoke a decision.

Day Fifteen: The Lasting Impact of Challenging Social Norms

Before Class:
- Complete your independent reading book. Bring the book to class.
- Bring both of the texts from different genres that you selected to analyze.

Key Learning Activities:
- Response: Today's lesson focus is "The lasting impact of challenging social norms." What kind of long-lasting impact do you think challenging social norms can have?
- Read aloud from *Bronx Masquerade*: "Tyrone" (pp. 162–165) and "Epilogue" (pp. 166–167).
- Response: Based on Tyrone's statement to the school at the assembly, what do you think is the lasting impact of Open Mike Fridays? Why do you think the poetry reading is important to Mai Tren?
- Follow-up discussion: How did the poems and reflections the students shared in Open Mike Fridays challenge social norms?
- Reflection: Select one of the texts you considered in this unit. What social norms are challenged in the text? What conclusions can reach about the potential lasting impact of challenging those social norms?
- Partner share: Share highlights from written responses.
- Whole-class discussion: What has stood out to you from this unit? What did it make you think about? What insights about challenging social norms will you take from it?
- Conversation: What are some benefits that can come from units like this one with an essential question and a range of texts related to that question? What did you think of the choices of texts in this unit?
- Discussion of the next day's final assessment workshop and work session.
- Exit question: What is something you learned in this unit about how and why people challenge social norms?

Key Standards Addressed:
- VA SOL 8.5: The student will read and analyze a variety of fictional texts, literary nonfiction, poetry, and drama.
- VA SOL 8.7: The student will write in a variety of forms to include narrative, expository, persuasive, and reflective with an emphasis on expository and persuasive writing.

- ◆ CCSS.ELA-LITERACY.RL.8.1: Cite the textual evidence that most strongly supports an analysis of what the text says explicitly as well as inferences drawn from the text.
- ◆ CCSS.ELA-LITERACY.RL.8.2: Determine a theme or central idea of a text and analyze its development over the course of the text, including its relationship to the characters, setting, and plot; provide an objective summary of the text.

Day Sixteen: Final Assessment Work Session

Before Class:
- ◆ Work on final unit assessment. Bring all drafts, outlines, ideas, and materials to class.

Key Learning Activities:
- ◆ Review of guidelines and rubric for final unit assessment.
- ◆ In-class work time on assessment.
- ◆ One-on-one conferences with teacher.
- ◆ Opportunities for peer feedback.
- ◆ Exit question: Describe the progress you made today on your assessment.

Key Standards Addressed:
- ◆ VA SOL 8.7: The student will write in a variety of forms to include narrative, expository, persuasive, and reflective with an emphasis on expository and persuasive writing.
- ◆ CCSS.ELA-LITERACY.W.8.1.B: Support claim(s) with logical reasoning and relevant evidence, using accurate, credible sources and demonstrating an understanding of the topic or text.
- ◆ CCSS.ELA-LITERACY.W.8.4: Produce clear and coherent writing in which the development, organization, and style are appropriate to task, purpose, and audience.
- ◆ CCSS.ELA-LITERACY.W.8.9: Draw evidence from literary or informational texts to support analysis, reflection, and research.

A note about this class meeting: If you want more time to confer with students, feel like they could benefit from extra in-class work time, or both, you may want to repeat this session to ensure students have the amount of support and time they need to successfully complete their assessments.

Day Seventeen: Final Assessment Publishing Celebration

Before Class:
◆ Complete final unit assessment. Bring a hard copy of your assessment for our publishing celebration and to turn in.

Key Learning Activities:
◆ Students share verbal summaries of the insights they shared in their assessments and the texts they selected.
◆ Assessment publishing celebration, in which students read one another's works and write positive comments on an attached sheet at the end of the piece.
◆ Exit question: What is something you read in a peer's assessment that impressed you?

Key Standards Addressed:
◆ VA SOL 8.7: The student will write in a variety of forms to include narrative, expository, persuasive, and reflective with an emphasis on expository and persuasive writing.
◆ CCSS.ELA-LITERACY.W.8.1.B: Support claim(s) with logical reasoning and relevant evidence, using accurate, credible sources and demonstrating an understanding of the topic or text.
◆ CCSS.ELA-LITERACY.W.8.4: Produce clear and coherent writing in which the development, organization, and style are appropriate to task, purpose, and audience.
◆ CCSS.ELA-LITERACY.W.8.9: Draw evidence from literary or informational texts to support analysis, reflection, and research.

Key Takeaway Ideas

- ◆ The goal of this chapter is to describe a form of inquiry-based literature instruction that merges the strengths of inquiry-oriented and essential-question-driven learning with the benefits of independent reading and student choice.
- ◆ In the unit discussed in this chapter that Sean taught to eighth-graders, students listened to, followed along with, and reflected on a read-aloud text related to the unit's essential question. They then selected independent reading books and texts of other genres that they connected to the essential question.
- ◆ This format, we feel, incorporates the same positive instructional features of the inquiry-based unit described in Chapter Three while also giving students the opportunity to make more decisions in the texts they read.
- ◆ As is the case for the example discussed in Chapter Three, the unit described in this chapter is intended to provide one model for how such a unit can look. While you can certainly teach this unit to your students in its current form, we also suggest that, as you reflect on the details of this unit, you think about how you might construct a unit that engages your students based on their interests and experiences.

Suggestions for Creating Your Own Unit

- ◆ The first step in the process of constructing a unit like this one is to craft an essential question. When creating the essential question for the unit described in this chapter, Sean wanted an inquiry-oriented question specific enough to apply to the read-aloud text, but still broad enough to enable students to consider a wide variety of works for their self-selected text sets. We suggest applying a similar framework when deciding on your essential question to maximize the instructional benefits of your unit.
- ◆ When crafting an essential question to use with your students, we suggest first thinking about the authentic interests they've expressed. Since a wonderful feature of inquiry-based learning is the way it provides opportunities for students to consider issues that matter to them, think about what topics are meaningful and relevant to their lives, and use those topics as the starting points for essential questions that will drive their inquiries. We suggest considering topics that seem to especially matter to students and asking them to complete questionnaires on ideas and issues that are particularly relevant to their lives.

◆ Once you've identified these topics, we suggest reflecting on key questions that relate to the topics, are open-ended, and require higher-order thinking skills to answer. These questions will facilitate strong and meaningful inquiry.

◆ After creating the essential question to use in your unit, we recommend deciding on a read-aloud text that aligns with the unit's essential question, relates to students' interests, and facilitates connections to other texts students will examine in the unit.

◆ To select a read-aloud text, we recommend reflecting on the unit's essential question and the issues and topics that are central to that question. Once you've identified those concepts, we suggest brainstorming and researching potential texts that address those topics and strike you as engaging and accessible to your students.

◆ When choosing a read-aloud, it's also important to keep in mind how well the book aligns with that form of presentation. For example, *Bronx Masquerade* worked well for Sean as a read-aloud because the format of the book is a series of personal narratives and corresponding poems—it aligns well with being read aloud. We've found that books that contain interesting dialogue and can be read expressively can work well as read-aloud text as these features align with exciting readings that hold students' attention.

◆ When students select their own texts, we recommend giving them freedom, but also providing them with supportive parameters and guidance. Sean asked students to select one independent reading book (fiction or nonfiction) and two texts from other genres (such as songs, poems, short stories, visual art, film, and nonfiction articles). He felt this provided students with an effective combination of freedom and support.

◆ To help students select these texts, we suggest first having students reflect on the unit's essential question and possible texts that align with it. Next, we recommend asking students to create potential text-set lists and annotations that describe texts they'd like to examine for the unit and how those texts align with the essential question. This process requires students to think carefully about the relationship between the texts they selected and the unit's essential question, thereby ensuring that students make well-informed choices regarding the works they select.

Resources and Reminders

◆ As with the unit described in Chapter Three, we recommend creating a unit rationale that you'll share with administrators, parents, and students to convey key features of the unit and orient all parties involved to its goals, procedures, benefits, and expectations. This document will convey to everyone involved that you've thought carefully about the inquiry-based attributes of this unit and promote an environment of clear and open communication. Through the rationale, you can illustrate why you've selected this approach and how it will positively impact students. We suggest using the rationale example in this chapter as a model to inform your work; while the details of your rationale will differ based on the features of your unit and local context, you can use the sections of the rationale to structure the ideas you'll share with parents, students, and administrators.

◆ We recommend constructing an assessment that is aligned with the unit's essential question and asks students to synthesize the texts they examined in the unit when reflecting on the essential question. When students consider all of the texts they examined and how those texts combine to inform their insights, they can understand that essential questions are multifaceted and have applicable to a range of texts and situations.

A Final Insight

◆ Inquiry-based units that incorporate student choice can provide engaging and thought-provoking opportunities for our students to think about complex and relevant topics. The ideas and examples described in this chapter will guide you as you put this instructional approach into action!

5

Connecting Genius Hour and Inquiry Through Student-Selected Inquiries

In this chapter, we'll discuss an approach to inquiry-based literature instruction that builds on the information and explanations of inquiry-based literature instruction previously described in this book. While Chapter Three described an inquiry-based unit with a class-wide essential question, assigned whole-class novel, and other texts read by all students, and Chapter Four provided additional freedom and flexibility for students by asking them to select independent reading texts and works from other genres that align with the class-wide essential question and read-aloud text, the unit detailed here in Chapter Five provides an additional level of student ownership. In this unit, which Sean taught to the same eighth-grade English class to which he taught the other units discussed in this book, students selected their areas of inquiry, created their own essential questions, and curated their own text sets that they felt would help them craft in-depth and multifaceted responses to those questions.

The student-centered structure and features of this unit are rooted in the principles of Genius Hour, which is a time dedicated to students' pursuits of their own passion projects (Krebs & Zvi, 2015). Genius Hour creates opportunities for students to ask driving questions about topics they care about, research answers to those questions, and share their responses (Coke, 2018); this unit incorporated those principles through its focus on students' areas of interest, questions related to those interests, and their selections and analyses of texts that aligned with the essential questions they created. The components of Genius Hour align perfectly with students' self-selected, multi-textual inquiries: through the process of designing a strong essential question and text set based on a high-interest topic, students are required to think carefully about what matters to them, what open-ended and thought-provoking questions about that topic they would like to investigate, and what texts could best help them generate and support thoughtful and complex responses.

The goal of this chapter is to describe a method of inquiry-based literature instruction that supports students as they design their own inquiry focuses, essential questions, and text sets. This approach, we feel, capitalizes on a key benefit of inquiry-oriented instruction: the opportunity for students to study issues, questions, and texts that especially matter to them. By doing so, we can further enhance students' feelings of agency, power, and freedom in their literature instruction. An eighth-grader in the class that Sean taught expressed the importance of these agency-related concepts, explaining "I really loved all of the freedom we had [in this unit]. I've never done anything like this in school where I could pick what I studied. It was like I was really free to learn about things I wanted to." The insights of education experts support this statement and further discuss the benefits of student-selected inquiry: in the book *Inquiry and Innovation in the Classroom: Using 20% Time, Genius Hour, and PBL to Drive Student Success*, author A.J. Juliani (2015) asserts, "Inquiry is the engine that drives innovation. When students are able to be curious, and explore their interests and passions, innovative work happens" (p. xvii). The information in this chapter is designed to help you guide your students as they engage in inquiry-oriented work that is driven by their interests, curiosities, and passions by showing you how Sean approached this form of instruction with his students and conveying key recommendations to consider in your own classroom.

We'll begin our exploration of student-selected inquiry units like the one Sean taught to his students by first considering how to introduce this type of unit to students and support them as they consider their areas of inquiry. Next, we'll reflect on how to help students think about and create essential questions related to their interests. Following that, we'll explore ways in which we as teachers can guide students through the process of selecting their own text sets that align with the essential questions they crafted. Then, we'll look closely at the rationale that Sean shared with administrators, students, and families before teaching this unit to eighth-graders. Once we've done that, we'll check out the assessment Sean asked his students to complete at the conclusion of the unit. Next, we'll see outlines of the daily lesson plans used in the unit. Finally, we'll look together at key takeaway ideas to consider when implementing this type of inquiry-based unit in your instruction.

As Sean's students navigated the process of creating their own inquiries, identifying areas of interest to them, crafting essential questions, and curating text sets aligned with those questions, Sean did the same alongside them.

He identified a big-picture topic he wanted to explore, created an essential question related to that topic, and decided on a text set that connected with that question. This practice allowed Sean to model key activities for students, such as turning an overarching concept into an essential question. In addition, throughout the unit, Sean talked with the students about the texts he was analyzing, which provided them with insight into how they could conduct their own analyses. You'll see examples of modeling and related instructional practices in this chapter.

The unit described in this chapter is a progression from the inquiry-based units detailed in Chapters Three and Four. Taken together, these three units represent a gradual release of responsibility to students (Pearson & Gallagher, 1983) by providing them with additional flexibility and agency throughout the units. We recommend implementing these three unit structures in sequence in order to maximize students' experiences with the possibilities and affordances of inquiry-based literature instruction. By progressing through these units, students can feel increasingly comfortable and familiar with inquiry-based literature instruction and the features of essential questions and varied text sets that draw on a number of genres. As you'll see in this unit, Sean frequently drew on the attributes and features of the units described in Chapters Three and Four when helping his students make decisions about their self-selected inquiry units. Now, let's get started on our exploration of this innovative unit!

Introducing the Unit

When you introduce this type of unit to your students, we recommend having a conversation with them that conveys how it is similar to and different from other inquiry-based units. For example, when Sean's students entered the classroom on the first day of this unit, he told them "Today, we're going to take our inquiry-based learning to a new level." He continued, "As you know, we've been working on inquiry-based units that are driven by essential questions. We're taking it to the next level now, because in the unit we're starting today, you're going to select your own topics, essential questions, and text sets."

Sean then talked with the students about the unit's key components, discussing how they would each be expected to select a topic, craft an essential question, and create a text set aligned with that question. After providing students with this overview information, Sean shared that the first step in this process would be identifying a topic or issue that would be the starting point for the rest of the selections they would make and the inquiry they would conduct: "When you think about your unit's topic, think in big-picture and general ways," Sean told his students. "Soon, we'll talk about creating essential questions related to the topic, but that's the next step. Today, we're thinking about big-picture topics that interest us."

After sharing these introductory statements with his students, Sean explained that they would be spending some time brainstorming big-picture topics that matter to them. "For example," he continued, "the first inquiry-based unit we did together was related to the big-picture topic of social action. The second one connected to the topic of societal norms. These are general topics that served as the starting points for our essential questions. Your job is to write in your response journals some big-picture and general topics that interest you."

When you guide your students through this process, we recommend giving them examples, as Sean did, of big-picture topics and how they can ultimately turn in to essential questions. This shows students the relationship between these unit components and helps them see the importance of brainstorming big-picture topics that will ultimately shape the rest of their work with this unit. In addition, we recommend modeling this activity for students by listing overarching issues and topics that matter to you and that you would like to explore further. This gives students insight into what the brainstorming process can be, which can inform their work as they do this on their own. For instance, before asking students to brainstorm on their own, Sean listed general topics on the whiteboard that he would like to investigate further, writing "community," "relationships," "support," and "identity."

Then, as students work independently on their own brainstorms, we suggest conferring with them individually. During these one-on-one check-ins, you can monitor students' progress and ensure that they understand the concept of big-picture ideas. For example, some students might not completely grasp the assignment and may therefore write more specific concepts or ideas, such as particular questions or observations about issues. If this happens, you can further explain the idea of exploring big-picture, general topics, using the examples you previously shared to guide their thinking. After all students have had sufficient time to brainstorm, they can share their ideas and potential topics with partners or in small groups, with volunteers then sharing their insights with the whole class.

Helping Students Create Essential Questions

Once students have considered possible overarching topics as the starting points for their self-selected inquiry units, their next step is to choose a topic and create an essential question that extends from that topic. When Sean taught this unit to his students, he devoted the unit's second day to talking with the students about the process of transitioning from a big-picture topic to a specific essential question that would guide their inquiry. To do this, he began by revisiting the previous day's class and connecting the large-scale ideas, such as "community," "relationships," "support," and "identity," discussed that day with the current day's focus of crafting an essential question. After reminding students of the previous day's focus, Sean transitioned to how those ideas represent starting points for the essential questions the students would create: "Today, we're going to take ideas we discussed yesterday and turn them into more specific essential questions," Sean told his students. "The big-picture ideas and topics we brainstormed in yesterday's class are the starting points for our units," he continued, "but for us to create our own inquiries, we need to create our own essential questions. Those questions will be what we'll try to answer during our inquiries."

Sean reminded the students of the essential questions that guided the two previous inquiry-based units—"What inspires individuals to take part in social action?" and "How and why do people challenge social norms?"—and talked with them about the attributes of those questions, asking them what they noticed about the questions and calling their attention to key features. "Remember that a good essential question is open-ended," Sean told his students. "It doesn't have one factual, specific answer that someone can just look up. A good essential question requires a lot of thinking, support, and analysis, like you did when responding to and reflecting on the essential questions in our last two inquiry-based units." When preparing your students to create their own essential questions, we recommend talking with them about the attributes of effective essential questions as Sean did with his students. In these conversations, it is a good idea to emphasize that the best questions are open-ended and create opportunities for in-depth reflection and analysis that is supported by a range of sources. (Chapter Two of this book, "Inquiry and Essential Questions," provides even more detailed explanation of the key components of essential questions.) You may also want to compare examples of questions that can work as strong essential questions with those that would not; for example, the essential questions discussed in Chapters Three and Four can facilitate authentic inquiry, while yes-no questions or those with specific, fact-based answers would not lend themselves to strong and engaging inquiry-based projects.

After you've talked with your students about these attributes of essential questions, we suggest asking them to pick one of the topics they brainstormed in the previous class and then working with them as they draft one or more essential questions related to that topic. Before Sean asked his students to do this, he modeled the practice for them, explaining that he had used the overarching ideas of "community," "relationships," "support," and "identity" to generate the essential question "What makes a strong community?" "This question came from the big-picture topics that interest me," he told his students. "I want to know more about communities and how they support individuals through things like relationships and valuing identities. Since I know good essential questions are open-ended and provide opportunities for a lot of analysis and critical thinking, I wanted to be sure that my question did this while still connecting to my interests."

While his students drafted essential questions related to the topic, Sean met with them individually to check on their progress. During these conferences, Sean ensured that the questions students drafted were open-ended and thought-provoking enough to drive their individual inquiries. If students' questions were too narrow or did not align with thoughtful analysis and support, Sean made suggestions to help the students craft questions that would work well for their units. As in the previous class in which students brainstormed their unit topics, students can share the questions they've brainstormed with groups or partners and volunteers can share with the whole class. Since essential questions are so important to the success of an inquiry-focused unit, Sean asked his students to give him a copy of the essential questions they would like to use for their individual units before they left class that day. He read those questions that evening, wrote feedback, and gave that feedback to students in the next class.

Guiding Students Through Text-Set Selection

Once students have identified essential questions that will drive their inquiries, they're ready to move to the next step of designing their own inquiry-based units: selecting the texts they'll use to answer their essential questions. One of the first steps in helping students with this selection process is to communicate the parameters of their selections. For example, when Sean conducted this unit with his eighth-graders, he asked them to select one book-length work and two texts from the genres of poetry, art, music, film, television, or another approved option. This structure resembled the textual components of the previous unit in which the students engaged (described in Chapter Four of this book), but, in this situation, the choices aligned with students' individually-created essential questions.

When Sean began talking with his students about selecting texts for their individual inquiries, he emphasized that the purpose of the unit text set is to have a variety of perspectives and types of works that help them answer their essential questions. "This text set should provide you with sources that you'll analyze and reflect on as your answer your unit's essential question," Sean told his students when preparing them to think about their text selections. "All of the texts you pick will be from different genres, but they'll have a very important common attribute: they'll all be related to your essential question and will help you answer it. Having a range of texts from different genres that are created by different authors, artists, filmmakers, poets, and other creators will make sure that you have a lot of points of view and ideas that will help you create an in-depth response to your question."

To begin the brainstorming process, Sean asked his students to write their essential question on a piece of paper and make three columns: books related to the question, texts of a different genre related to the question, and texts of another genre. (The texts in the second and third columns should represent different genres.) He then asked them to research texts that they thought had the potential to inform their thinking related to the question and fill out the columns accordingly. "Write several options in your columns as you research potential texts," Sean told his students. "Once you have those written, you can think carefully about the different options and then identify the texts that you'd like to select for your unit text set."

Sean modeled this activity, listing the essential question "What makes a strong community?" on the top of a page projected to the front of the room using a document camera. He then listed books, songs, paintings, photographs, and films that he thought had the potential to align well with and inform this question. Students found the brainstorming method to be a helpful way to consider potential texts since it provided a concrete framework to support their selections. Since the process of text selection can be overwhelming if students are not given concrete parameters and support, we recommend providing students with specific guidelines for text selection and with brainstorming tactics to guide them as they considered potential texts.

As students work independently to brainstorm these possibilities, we suggest holding one-on-one conferences with them to discuss their ideas and answer questions they have. During these conversations, an effective tactic is to ask students to talk to you about how texts they've selected relate to their essential questions. By asking students to explain the relationship between their questions and the texts they're considering, you can gauge their understandings and provide them with support when necessary. When conducting these conferences with his students, Sean enjoyed hearing how the students connected their questions with possible texts and asked them clarifying questions when relevant to help the students develop their explanations of how certain texts aligned with their essential questions. In addition, when students had difficulty thinking of some potential texts (such as those from various genres, for example), Sean was able to offer ideas and suggestions of possible choices for them to consider.

After students take the majority of the class period to consider potential text sets, we recommend asking them to conclude the day's session by sharing with small-group members highlights of their explorations and brainstorms. In these conversations, students can talk to their peers about the texts they have considered and how these texts align with their individual unit questions. One benefit of this practice is that peers are sometimes well-positioned to recommend and describe contemporary, high-interest texts that their classmates can consider for inclusion in their units. For example, several of Sean's students recommended contemporary songs to their peers that closely aligned with the essential questions those students had identified.

For homework that night, Sean asked his students to finalize their text-set selections by creating a document that listed the three texts they would like to use for their units and provided annotations for each text. In this document, students identified the books they wanted to use for the unit and the two other texts from different genres. When writing the annotation for each work, the students described the piece and discussed how it relates to the unit's essential question. To support students as they did this, Sean shared with them an example set list annotation that he created for the unit he constructed. This document identified the texts Sean selected for his inquiry unit and described how each of those texts aligned with the question "What makes a strong community?" For this inquiry, Sean selected the novel *Miracle's Boys* by Jacqueline Woodson, the *New York Times* article "What the Arlee Warriors Were Playing For" by Abe Streep about high school basketball players on Montana's Flathead Indian Reservation, and the song "The Show Goes On" by Lupe Fiasco. Using this example annotation as a model, students brought the document they created to Sean at the beginning of the next day's class. After he reviewed and approved the text sets and annotations, students were able to get started reading and analyzing their texts.

The process of students crafting their own text sets to correspond with essential questions they've identified is nuanced and potentially challenging, but is also extremely rewarding in the way it facilitates student-driven inquiries and provides students with a unique sense of agency made possible by this type of instruction. One tactic that Sean utilized with his students that worked especially well during this unit was to organize the class into "table groups" of four or five students. The students in these table groups talked together about their texts and inquiries throughout the unit before Sean asked for volunteers to share with the whole class. By talking with their table-group members about their ideas, students had opportunities to share their inquiry findings with a consistent set of individuals and to learn a great deal from one another's inquiries. Sean combined these table-group conversations with whole-class discussions to allow for a range of opportunities that students could utilize when sharing with and learning from each other.

Now that we've explored ideas regarding introducing this unit to students, helping them create essential questions, and guiding them through their text-set selections, let's look in the next section at the unit rationale that Sean created to describe the important features of this unit.

Rationale

Like the rationale examples featured in Chapters Three and Four, this section contains the rationale that Sean shared with administrators, students, and families before he taught this unit in order to give everyone involved a complete understanding of the key attributes and benefits of this unit. Since the unit described in this chapter is especially innovative, student-centered, and potentially unfamiliar to many, it's particularly important to communicate to all parties involved the merits of its instructional and organizational features. Rationales such as this one can go a long way in creating strong lines of communication with students' families, school administrators, and with our students themselves. They keep everyone aware of important instructional practices and can eliminate questions or confusion later in the unit due to their proactive nature. Because of this, we encourage you to use this rationale as a model for one that you'll create to share with interested parties when you teach units like this one to your students. We describe some suggestions about unit rationales to consider in the "Key Takeaway Ideas" section at the end of this chapter.

This document describes the unit that Sean Ruday will be working on with his eighth-grade English class. It provides a rationale for the unit by identifying and describing four of its key aspects: 1) the unit's focus, 2) the unit's key attributes, 3) the unit's connection to educational objectives, and 4) the unit's relevance to students' needs. By reading this document, you'll gain an understanding of the unit's most important features and strengths.

The Unit's Focus
This unit focuses on students engaging in inquiry-based learning that centers their interests and curiosities. It builds off of the previous two inquiry-based units in which students engaged, giving them even more freedom than they had in those units to explore their interests. While, in the previous two units, students were given teacher-created essential questions to which they would respond, this unit asks students to craft their own essential questions and

generate their own text sets that correspond with that question. After students design their essential questions and text sets, they will do a great deal of discussion and analysis of how the texts they selected inform their individually selected questions. Through the unit's student-centered structure and opportunities for interaction and analysis, students will be able to explore questions that matter to them, analyzing a range of texts while doing so.

The Unit's Key Attributes

Two especially important attributes of this unit are the text sets that the students create and engage with throughout the unit and the assessments that the students will complete at the unit's conclusion. These components are essential to the students' experiences analyzing and reflecting on the inquiries identified in their essential questions. There are other components of the unit that will certainly impact students' learning experiences, such as the small-group and whole-class discussions they will have about their inquiries and the informal written reflections students will complete throughout the unit. However, this section focuses on the student-created text set and its assessment due to their central role in the unit.

The text set that students create for this unit will align with the essential questions that they individually construct. For these text sets, each student will select one fiction or nonfiction book that aligns with their essential question. In addition, each student will select two texts from other genres, such as poetry, art, music, film, television, or another approved option. Through a combination of teacher guidance, student brainstorming, and peer support, students will create proposed text-set lists for their units. They will share these proposals with Sean; once he approves them, the students will be able to get started analyzing these texts. Then, students will reflect throughout the unit on how the texts they've selected align with their essential questions. This text-selection structure resembles the components of the preceding unit, but that unit involved a teacher-created essential question and class-wide read-aloud text. In this unit, both the essential questions and text sets will be created by individual students to maximize their agency and ensure their abilities to explore topics and ideas that interest them.

The assessment that students will complete at the end of this unit asks students to write a reflective essay that uses all three of the works in their text set to respond to the essential question they chose to investigate. In this essay, students will synthesize the texts they've analyzed during the unit and use their insights to answer their essential question. For example, Sean is investigating the essential question "What makes a strong community?" in an inquiry that he will conduct while the students conduct their own. In the final assessment, he would answer that question by answering that question and supporting his response with the texts they analyzed during the unit. This project will challenge students by asking them to consider similarities and differences in the ways the works in their text sets addressed their focal topic and then requiring them to use the ideas in those texts to form a cohesive response to a challenging and nuanced question. This process will enable students to benefit from the in-depth learning and higher-order thinking associated with inquiry-based instruction. The recommended length of this reflective essay is three to four pages.

The Unit's Connection to Educational Objectives

This unit's student-centered, inquiry-driven, and multifaceted approach closely aligns with rigorous and current educational objectives that prioritize students' interpretations and syntheses of a range of works across various genres. The variety of genres represented in the student-created text sets and the interpretive work the students will do with those pieces will prepare them for the comparison-based analysis prioritized by the paired-passage text-dependent questions required by the most recent Virginia Standards of Learning for English, in which students analyze paired works of different genres that focus on similar topics. [*Note to readers of this book: This unit, like the others described in this book was taught in Virginia.*]

In addition, the unit's features, including its range of texts and focus on in-depth analysis and comparison, result in its alignment with many important state and national standards for eighth-grade students.

Some especially relevant Virginia Standards of Learning are:

- ◆ VA SOL 8.5: The student will read and analyze a variety of fictional texts, literary nonfiction, poetry, and drama.
- ◆ VA SOL 8.7: The student will write in a variety of forms to include narrative, expository, persuasive, and reflective with an emphasis on expository and persuasive writing.
                              (Virginia Department of Education, 2017)

Viewed from a national perspective, this unit's components connect it with many Common Core State Standards, such as those listed below:

- ◆ CCSS.ELA-LITERACY.W.8.1.B: Support claim(s) with logical reasoning and relevant evidence, using accurate, credible sources and demonstrating an understanding of the topic or text.
- ◆ CCSS.ELA-LITERACY.W.8.4: Produce clear and coherent writing in which the development, organization, and style are appropriate to task, purpose, and audience.

- ◆ CCSS.ELA-LITERACY.W.8.9: Draw evidence from literary or informational texts to support analysis, reflection, and research.
- ◆ CCSS.ELA-LITERACY.RL.8.1: Cite the textual evidence that most strongly supports an analysis of what the text says explicitly as well as inferences drawn from the text.
- ◆ CCSS.ELA-LITERACY.RL.8.2: Determine a theme or central idea of a text and analyze its development over the course of the text, including its relationship to the characters, setting, and plot; provide an objective summary of the text.
- ◆ CCSS.ELA-LITERACY.RL.8.3: Analyze how particular lines of dialogue or incidents in a story or drama propel the action, reveal aspects of a character, or provoke a decision.

(Common Core State Standards Initiative, 2010)

These standards illustrate the rigor and benefits connected with the inquiry and analysis that are central to this unit. The thought-provoking, essential-question-driven, and multi-textual components of the unit will provide students with learning experiences that align with a variety of important academic standards.

[*Note to readers of this book: As we have discussed throughout this book, an excellent aspect of inquiry-based learning is its alignment with so many learning goals and standards. Since inquiry facilitates rigorous and in-depth analysis, it is easy to assure all interested parties that students will be participating in instruction that aligns with educational objectives reflected in many sets of standards and learning goals. We recommend examining the specific standards in your state and identifying ways those objectives align with the features of the unit and inquiry-based literature instruction, as Sean did in this rationale.*]

The Unit's Relevance to Students' Needs

In addition to meeting important academic standards, this unit provides excellent opportunities for students to do engaging work that is relevant to them in personal and academic ways. This section describes three ways that this unit relates to students' academic and social needs.

1. This unit can help students explore topics that matter to them personally.
   The individualized essential questions that students investigate in this unit allow them to explore issues that matter to them, creating authentic connections to their individual identities and experiences. A number of students have expressed their beliefs that school in general lacks relevance and meaning to their lives—which is an idea supported by the work of researchers such as Duncan-Andrade and Morrell (2005)

who explore the importance of curriculum that is meaningful to students and relevant to their experiences. By crafting essential questions that address issues related to their lives and interests, students can design their inquiries to align with their authentic interests.

2. The unit calls for students to select and synthesize a wide cross-section of texts and genres.

Many rigorous state and national standards prioritize students' abilities to understand, interpret, and synthesize the ideas in a wide range of texts. This unit aligns with those academic objectives perfectly, as it requires students to carefully and intentionally select texts that align with a similar theme and then synthesize how those works address that theme. The processes of text selection, interpretation, and synthesis in which students will engage in this unit will help them achieve academic objectives that value these challenging and thought-provoking comparison-based concepts. In contrast to other forms of literature instruction that focus only on a single text without considering how it connects to other works, this unit's format will build students' abilities to think about, reflect on, and synthesize important similarities and key distinctions in the texts they'll select and utilize.

3. The unit requires students to create well-informed conclusions about meaningful topics.

This unit not only calls for students to select topics and issues that matter to them and synthesize work addressing those topics, but also requires them to create well-informed and carefully constructed conclusions about those issues. Given the amount of information available in today's society through a range of platforms and resources, it is especially important that students are able to think carefully about topics in which they are interested and construct well-informed conclusions based on evidence and insights from a range of sources. When conducting analyses of their text sets throughout the unit and using those insights to create their responses to the final assessment, students will gain experiences constructing informed conclusions about topics that are current, relevant, and meaningful to them. Their abilities to put together these well-informed insights will serve them well in a wide range of contexts—in school, in their careers, and in their everyday lives.

Sean is greatly looking forward to working with the students as they engage with this unit. He believes that its authentic opportunities for inquiry, agency, and analysis represent the best practices of English instruction. In addition to achieving important educational objectives, it can engage and empower students, helping them develop key skills and ideas that will serve them well in school and beyond. Sean is happy to talk further about this unit and encourages you to contact him at sean.ruday@gmail.com with any questions or comments.

Assessment

This section describes the assessment that Sean's students completed at the end of the self-selected inquiry unit. It contains the assessment description Sean distributed to his students and the rubric he used when evaluating students' works. In this assessment, students were asked to write a reflective essay that used all three of the works in their text set to respond to the essential question they chose to investigate, synthesizing the texts they've analyzed during the unit and use their insights to answer their essential question. The choice and structure of this assessment extended naturally from the instructional freedom and agency that this unit facilitated. When engaging your students in inquiry-based instruction that asks them to construct their own essential questions and text sets, we recommend giving them assessments that provide them with opportunities to reflect on the questions they created using the text sets they designed. We also suggest sharing the assessment description very early in the unit and providing your students with the evaluation criteria at that time. You can find additional assessment information in the "Key Takeaway Ideas" section later in this chapter and in Chapter Six, "Assessing Inquiry."

Assessment Description Distributed to Students

For this unit's assessment, you will write a reflective essay that answers the essential question you created for your inquiry. In this essay, you will analyze the three texts you selected for your text set and use the information from those sources and your understandings of them to support your response. Since this unit is individualized to your specific essential questions and text sets, the particular topics and texts you'll address in your assessment will be individualized also. You'll answer your essential questions and use your text sets to do so; the specifics of your responses will depend on the question each one of you created and the corresponding text set. No matter what your individual questions and text sets are, you will analyze those works by identifying similarities and differences in the ways they address your essential question and use them to form a well-developed response to that question.

You will need to cite these texts directly in your essay and describe how they inform your response to your essential question. (You will also cite them in a Works Cited page following the reflection.) The recommended length of your reflection is three to four typed pages in Times New Roman, double-spaced, not including the Works Cited page. I will hold individual conferences with you as you write this piece. I am happy to answer any questions you have and am very excited to see what you create!

Assessment Rubric

STUDENT-SELECTED INQUIRY UNIT ASSESSMENT RUBRIC

Criteria	1	2	3	4	Feedback
Insights • Does the author's response provide thoughtful insights that address the essential question they created? • Are these insights clear, specific, and detailed? • Do the author's points convey a deep and nuanced understanding of the essential question?					
Textual support • Are the author's insights supported with specific and detailed connections to the works in the text set they created and studied? • Does the author effectively communicate the relationship between these texts and the unit's essential question? • Is it clear that the author has carefully analyzed these texts with the unit's essential question in mind?					
Organization • Is the paper clearly organized? • Are paragraphs used in the paper's organization? • Is it clear when the author moves from one "train of thought" to another?					
Mechanics • Does the writing utilize proper mechanics? • Does it demonstrate an understanding of proper punctuation? • Are sentences clear and representative of complete thoughts? • Is capitalization used at appropriate times?					

1-criteria not met;   2-criteria partially met;   3-criteria met;   4-criteria exceeded

Total score:
Overall feedback:

Daily Lesson Plans

This section contains outlines of the daily lesson plans Sean used in this unit. Each day's description lists the day's focus, any work done before class, the main learning activities, and key state and national standards addressed in the day's lesson. These lesson plan outlines provide an example of what an inquiry-based unit that features student-created essential questions and text sets can look like. We suggest using these plan outlines to inform your work as you create similar units for your students!

Day One: Introducing the Unit and Its Big-Picture Topics

Key Learning Activities:
- Discussion of unit features.
- Class conversation on the importance of big-picture topics to self-constructed essential questions.
- Model brainstorm of big-picture topics.
- Students brainstorm their big-picture topics.
- Small-group share of students' big-picture topics.
- Whole-class share of students' big-picture topics.
- Exit question: Why is thinking about big-picture topics that matter to you important to construct your own inquiry-based unit?

Key Standards Addressed:
- VA SOL 8.7: The student will write in a variety of forms to include narrative, expository, persuasive, and reflective with an emphasis on expository and persuasive writing.
- CCSS.ELA-LITERACY.W.8.4: Produce clear and coherent writing in which the development, organization, and style are appropriate to task, purpose, and audience.

Day Two: Helping Students Create Essential Questions

Key Learning Activities:
- Review of big-picture topics.
- Connection between big-picture topics and essential questions.
- Discussion of key attributes of effective essential questions, including Sean's model essential question.

- Comparison of strong essential questions and less-effective ones.
- Students brainstorm essential questions using big-picture topics from previous class as starting points.
- Teacher and students hold individual conferences about students' essential questions.
- Small-group share of students' essential question drafts.
- Whole class share of students' essential question drafts.
- Students give teacher their essential question drafts. The teacher will provide feedback on the question draft.
- Exit question: What is an attribute of a strong essential question? How does your essential question draft exemplify that attribute?

Key Standards Addressed:
- VA SOL 8.7: The student will write in a variety of forms to include narrative, expository, persuasive, and reflective with an emphasis on expository and persuasive writing.
- CCSS.ELA-LITERACY.W.8.4: Produce clear and coherent writing in which the development, organization, and style are appropriate to task, purpose, and audience.

Day Three: Guiding Students Through Text-Set Selection

Key Learning Activities:
- Introduction of final unit assessment.
- Overview of the unit's text-set features.
- Discussion: The purpose of text sets in inquiry-based instruction.
- Mini-lesson with examples: How text sets align with essential questions.
- Brainstorm and research: Consider and investigate multiple options of potential texts that correspond with your essential question.
- Teacher and students hold individual conferences about students' text-set ideas focusing on how the potential texts relate to the essential question.

- ◆ Small-group share of students' text-set brainstorms and explorations.
- ◆ Whole-class share of students' text-set brainstorms and explorations.
- ◆ Discussion of model text-set annotation.
- ◆ Exit question: What is one text in your text set that you are especially excited to analyze? How does it connect to your essential question?

Key Standards Addressed:
- ◆ VA SOL 8.5: The student will read and analyze a variety of fictional texts, literary nonfiction, poetry, and drama.
- ◆ VA SOL 8.7: The student will write in a variety of forms to include narrative, expository, persuasive, and reflective with an emphasis on expository and persuasive writing.
- ◆ CCSS.ELA-LITERACY.RL.8.1: Cite the textual evidence that most strongly supports an analysis of what the text says explicitly as well as inferences drawn from the text.
- ◆ CCSS.ELA-LITERACY.RL.8.2: Determine a theme or central idea of a text and analyze its development over the course of the text, including its relationship to the characters, setting, and plot; provide an objective summary of the text.

Day Four: Beginning to Make Connections

Before class: Create a potential text set list and corresponding set of annotations: List the three texts you would like to use for your unit and provide an annotation for each. In the annotation for each text, describe the piece and discuss how it relates to your unit's essential question. Bring your proposed book-length text to class.

Key Learning Activities:
- ◆ Shared reading: Opening section of "What the Arlee Warriors Were Playing For."
- ◆ Think aloud: Sean makes connections between this article excerpt and the essential question of his self-selected inquiry.
- ◆ Sean meets with students to discuss their text sets. Students begin reading the book in their text sets when the set is approved. Revision suggestions to text sets made as needed.

- Response: Students make connections between what they read during the reading time and the essential questions of their individual inquiries.
- Small-group discussion: Students share their responses with their table groups.
- Follow-up response: Students return to the reading they did earlier in the day's class and identify an excerpt that especially connects with their essential questions.
- Sharing: Students share their excerpts and reflections with partners. Volunteers share responses with the whole class.
- Exit question: What is a way the text you read today connected with your essential question?

Key Standards Addressed:
- VA SOL 8.5: The student will read and analyze a variety of fictional texts, literary nonfiction, poetry, and drama.
- VA SOL 8.7: The student will write in a variety of forms to include narrative, expository, persuasive, and reflective with an emphasis on expository and persuasive writing.
- CCSS.ELA-LITERACY.RL.8.1: Cite the textual evidence that most strongly supports an analysis of what the text says explicitly as well as inferences drawn from the text.
- CCSS.ELA-LITERACY.RL.8.3: Analyze how particular lines of dialogue or incidents in a story or drama propel the action, reveal aspects of a character, or provoke a decision.

Day Five: Creating Deeper Connections

Before Class:
- Read book-length text for 20 minutes.
- Bring all three works in your text set to class.

Key Learning Activities:
- Shared listening and reading: "The Show Goes On."
- Think aloud: Sean connects the way "The Show Goes On" relates to the essential question to the way the other two texts in the unit relate to it.

- ◆ Model reflection: Sean lists his essential question on the top of a piece of paper. In three columns underneath that question, he notes ways each text has informed his understanding of his essential question so far.
- ◆ Follow-up: Students complete their own versions of the reflection as Sean confers with them.
- ◆ Mini-lesson: Sean reads a passage from *Miracle's Boys* and describes how it helps him think further about his essential question.
- ◆ Independent reading: Students read their book-length texts and make additional notes about how the text informs their understandings of their essential questions.
- ◆ Small-group discussion: Students share with their table groups their responses from their reflections, focusing on how each text has informed their understandings of their essential questions.
- ◆ Whole-class share: Volunteers share highlights from their responses with the whole class.
- ◆ Follow-up response: Students return to the reading they did earlier in the day's class and identify an excerpt that especially connects with their essential questions.
- ◆ Sharing: Students share their excerpts and reflections with partners. Volunteers share responses with the whole class.
- ◆ Exit prompt: Select one of the texts in your text set and write how it has informed your understanding of your essential question so far.

Key Standards Addressed:
- ◆ VA SOL 8.5: The student will read and analyze a variety of fictional texts, literary nonfiction, poetry, and drama.
- ◆ VA SOL 8.7: The student will write in a variety of forms to include narrative, expository, persuasive, and reflective with an emphasis on expository and persuasive writing.
- ◆ CCSS.ELA-LITERACY.RL.8.2: Determine a theme or central idea of a text and analyze its development over the course of the text, including its relationship to the characters, setting, and plot; provide an objective summary of the text.
- ◆ CCSS.ELA-LITERACY.RL.8.3: Analyze how particular lines of dialogue or incidents in a story or drama propel the action, reveal aspects of a character, or provoke a decision.

Day Six: Considering Specific Textual Excerpts and Essential Questions

Before Class:
- ◆ Read book-length text for 20 minutes.
- ◆ Bring all three works in your text set to class.

Key Learning Activities:
- ◆ Mini-lesson: Using specific textual excerpts to inform essential questions.
- ◆ Model activity: Sean models completion of a graphic organizer that asks the student to identify a line from each text in the text set that aligns with the essential question and explain the connection between that line and the essential question.
- ◆ Follow-up: Students complete graphic organizers, identifying lines from their texts that connect to their questions while Sean confers with them and monitors their progress.
- ◆ Small-group share: Students share their text excerpts and insights with their table groups.
- ◆ Whole-class share: Volunteers share excerpts and insights with the whole class.
- ◆ Read aloud/think aloud: Sean reads another passage from *Miracle's Boys*, identifies a line that connects to his unit's essential question, and describes why the line relates to the question.
- ◆ Independent reading: Students read their book-length texts and write in their response journals lines that connect their essential questions and why those lines relate to the question.
- ◆ Small-group share: Students share a line they identified with their table groups as well as why that line connects with their essential questions.
- ◆ Whole-class share: Volunteers share identified lines and insights with the whole class.
- ◆ Exit question: How do you think looking at specific excerpts from texts can help us respond to our essential questions? Support your response with connections to our work today.

Key Standards Addressed:
- ◆ VA SOL 8.5: The student will read and analyze a variety of fictional texts, literary nonfiction, poetry, and drama.

- VA SOL 8.7: The student will write in a variety of forms to include narrative, expository, persuasive, and reflective with an emphasis on expository and persuasive writing.
- CCSS.ELA-LITERACY.RL.8.1: Cite the textual evidence that most strongly supports an analysis of what the text says explicitly as well as inferences drawn from the text.
- CCSS.ELA-LITERACY.RL.8.3: Analyze how particular lines of dialogue or incidents in a story or drama propel the action, reveal aspects of a character, or provoke a decision.

Day Seven: Reflecting on How Genres Facilitate Messages

Before Class:
- Read book-length text for 20 minutes.
- Bring all three works in your text set to class.

Key Learning Activities:
- Mini-lesson: Genre features and how they help creators deliver messages.
- Model activity: Sean reflects on the different genres of the works in his text set. He models completion of a reflection activity that asks students to think about the features of each genre and how each piece's genre features help convey its message.
- Follow-up: Students complete the reflection activity, recording their insights on how the genre features of each piece in their text set help convey the piece's message and inform their understandings of their essential questions. Sean confers with students while they do this.
- Small-group share: Students share their reflections with their table groups.
- Whole-class share: Volunteers share reflections with the whole class.
- Read-aloud/think-aloud: Sean reads a passage from *Miracle's Boys* and thinks aloud about how the key ideas in that passage might look if they were in a different genre, such as a song, painting, or poem.
- Independent reading and reflection: Students read their book-length texts and identify a key idea in that passage. They then reflect on how the key idea in that passage might look if it was expressed through a different genre. Sean confers with students as they create their reflections.

◆ Small-group share: Students share with their table groups the reflections they completed during independent reading.

◆ Whole-class share: Volunteers share their reflections with the whole class.

◆ Exit question: Based on our activities and discussions today, what role do you think genre plays in the ways text share messages and ideas with their audiences?

Key Standards Addressed:

◆ VA SOL 8.5: The student will read and analyze a variety of fictional texts, literary nonfiction, poetry, and drama.

◆ VA SOL 8.7: The student will write in a variety of forms to include narrative, expository, persuasive, and reflective with an emphasis on expository and persuasive writing.

◆ CCSS.ELA-LITERACY.RL.8.1: Cite the textual evidence that most strongly supports an analysis of what the text says explicitly as well as inferences drawn from the text.

◆ CCSS.ELA-LITERACY.RL.8.2: Determine a theme or central idea of a text and analyze its development over the course of the text, including its relationship to the characters, setting, and plot; provide an objective summary of the text.

Day Eight: Examining Key Distinctions Between the Works in our Text Sets

Before Class:

◆ Read book-length text for 20 minutes.

◆ Bring all three works in your text set to class.

Key Learning Activities:

◆ Mini-lesson: Synthesis and analysis. This mini-lesson focuses on why it's not only important to identify similarities between works in our text sets, but also key differences in those works and the ways they address key concepts.

◆ Model activity: Sean models an analysis of the works in his text set, discussing how, even though the works address the same essential question, they provide different insights into that question. He completes a graphic organizer that asks for the unit's essential question, the works' titles, and the different ways each text addresses the essential question.

◆ Follow-up: Students complete the analysis activity, using a graphic organizer to record their thoughts on different ways each of the texts in their text sets addresses the essential question. Sean confers with students as they do this.

◆ Small-group share: Students share their analyses with their table groups.

◆ Whole-class share: Volunteers share their analyses with the class.

◆ Read-aloud/think-aloud: Sean reads a passage from *Miracle's Boys*, thinking aloud about how the passage addresses his unit's essential question and how it addresses that question differently than the other texts in his text set do.

◆ Independent reading and reflection: Students read their book-length texts. In their response journals, each student identifies a passage that connects to the essential question, discusses how the passage aligns with the question and how it addresses the question differently than the other two texts in the student's text set do.

◆ Small-group share: Students share with their table groups the reflections they completed during independent reading.

◆ Whole-class share: Volunteers share their reflections with the whole class.

◆ Exit question: Based on our activities and discussions today, why do you think it's important to think about the different ways the works in our text sets address our essential questions?

Key Standards Addressed:

◆ VA SOL 8.5: The student will read and analyze a variety of fictional texts, literary nonfiction, poetry, and drama.

◆ VA SOL 8.7: The student will write in a variety of forms to include narrative, expository, persuasive, and reflective with an emphasis on expository and persuasive writing.

◆ CCSS.ELA-LITERACY.RL.8.1: Cite the textual evidence that most strongly supports an analysis of what the text says explicitly as well as inferences drawn from the text.

◆ CCSS.ELA-LITERACY.W.8.9: Draw evidence from literary or informational texts to support analysis, reflection, and research.

Day Nine: What We Know and What Questions We Have

Before Class:
◆ Read book-length text for 20 minutes.
◆ Bring all three works in your text set to class.

Key Learning Activities:
◆ Mini-lesson: The importance of considering what we know and what questions we have, focusing on the significance of continued questioning to successfully completing an inquiry.
◆ Model activity: Sean demonstrates the questioning process described in the mini-lesson by listing three things he's learned so far about his essential question during this inquiry and three questions he still has.
◆ Follow-up: Students complete this activity on their own, identifying three things they've learned about their essential questions and three questions they have. Sean confers with students while they do this, monitoring their progress and supporting them as they compose their questions.
◆ Small-group share: Students share their responses with their table groups.
◆ Whole-class share: Volunteers share highlights of their responses with the class.
◆ Independent analysis and writing: Students use their text sets to reflect on, analyze, and respond to as many of the questions they created as possible. Sean meets with students to support them as they do this.
◆ Small-group share: Students share the answers they created during the independent work time.
◆ Whole-class share: Volunteers share one question they answered during the independent work time and how they answered it.
◆ Exit question: What is something you learned about your inquiry through creating and responding to questions you have?

Key Standards Addressed:
◆ VA SOL 8.5: The student will read and analyze a variety of fictional texts, literary nonfiction, poetry, and drama.
◆ VA SOL 8.7: The student will write in a variety of forms to include narrative, expository, persuasive, and reflective with an emphasis on expository and persuasive writing.

◆ CCSS.ELA-LITERACY.RL.8.1: Cite the textual evidence that most strongly supports an analysis of what the text says explicitly as well as inferences drawn from the text.
◆ CCSS.ELA-LITERACY.W.8.9: Draw evidence from literary or informational texts to support analysis, reflection, and research.

Day Ten: Considering What Has Surprised Us

Before Class:
◆ Read book-length text for 20 minutes.
◆ Bring all three works in your text set to class.
◆ Complete your responses to the questions you began answering in Day Nine's class.

Key Learning Activities:
◆ Mini-lesson: What has surprised us in our inquiries. Sean conducts a mini-lesson on the reflective process of what has stood out to and surprised the class members as they've conducted their individual inquiries. In this lesson, he focuses on the importance of thinking about what has surprised us and using those insights to inform our inquiries.
◆ Model activity: Sean models a reflection in which he thinks aloud about and writes down what has surprised him so far during his inquiry, why it has stood out to him, and how those ideas can inform his response to his essential question.
◆ Follow-up response: Students complete the reflection Sean modeled, noting what has surprised them so far during their inquiries, why those insights have surprised them, and how those ideas can inform their responses to their essential questions. Sean confers with students as they work, supporting them as he can.
◆ Small-group share: Students share their reflections with their table groups.
◆ Whole-class share: Volunteers share highlights of their reflections with the class.
◆ Read-aloud/think-aloud: Sean reads a passage from *Miracle's Boys* and identifies a line from it. He indicates what he can infer

from that line and how it informs his understanding of his essential question.

◆ Independent reading and response: Students read their book-length texts. In their response journals, each student identifies a line from their book. As Sean modeled, they then indicate what they can infer from that line and how it informs their understanding of the essential question.

◆ Small-group share: Students share with their table groups the responses they completed during independent reading.

◆ Whole-class share: Volunteers share their responses with the whole class.

◆ Exit question: What is something that has especially surprised you as you've conducted your inquiry?

Key Standards Addressed:
◆ VA SOL 8.5: The student will read and analyze a variety of fictional texts, literary nonfiction, poetry, and drama.

◆ VA SOL 8.7: The student will write in a variety of forms to include narrative, expository, persuasive, and reflective with an emphasis on expository and persuasive writing.

◆ CCSS.ELA-LITERACY.RL.8.1: Cite the textual evidence that most strongly supports an analysis of what the text says explicitly as well as inferences drawn from the text.

◆ CCSS.ELA-LITERACY.RL.8.3: Analyze how particular lines of dialogue or incidents in a story or drama propel the action, reveal aspects of a character, or provoke a decision.

◆ CCSS.ELA-LITERACY.W.8.9: Draw evidence from literary or informational texts to support analysis, reflection, and research.

Day Eleven: Identifying Key Themes

Before Class:
◆ Read book-length text for 20 minutes.
◆ Bring all three works in your text set to class.

Key Learning Activities:
◆ Mini-lesson: Identifying key themes and concepts in our inquiries. Sean conducts a mini-lesson that focuses on the

identification of key themes and concepts in an inquiry. To do this, he describes what it means to identify overarching themes that are supported by evidence and discusses how this aligns with strong inquiry and analysis.

◆ Model activity: Sean models the process of identifying three key themes from his inquiry, noting important concepts that have emerged from his experience analyzing his text set and considering his essential question. He describes how he identifies those themes and information that supports the identification, using a graphic organizer to do so.

◆ Follow-up: Students work on the activity Sean modeled, completing a graphic organizer that asks them to identify three key themes that they've noticed from their inquiries and information that supports each theme identification. Sean confers with students as they do this, supporting them and asking follow-up questions.

◆ Small-group share: Students share their themes and explanations associated with those themes with their table groups.

◆ Whole-class share: Volunteers share their themes and explanations with the whole class.

◆ Read-aloud/think-aloud: Sean reads aloud passage from *Miracle's Boys* and thinks aloud about how parts of the passage support the themes he's identified and how others help him also consider a new theme.

◆ Independent reading: Students read their book-length works, writing in their response journals how the information they read aligns with the themes they noted or helps them consider new themes.

◆ Small-group share: Students share with their table groups the responses they completed during independent reading.

◆ Whole-class share: Volunteers share their responses with the whole class.

◆ Exit question: What is one of the themes you considered today that especially stands out to you as important to your response to your unit's essential question?

Key Standards Addressed:

◆ VA SOL 8.5: The student will read and analyze a variety of fictional texts, literary nonfiction, poetry, and drama.

◆ VA SOL 8.7: The student will write in a variety of forms to include narrative, expository, persuasive, and reflective with an emphasis on expository and persuasive writing.

◆ CCSS.ELA-LITERACY.RL.8.1: Cite the textual evidence that most strongly supports an analysis of what the text says explicitly as well as inferences drawn from the text.

◆ CCSS.ELA-LITERACY.RL.8.2: Determine a theme or central idea of a text and analyze its development over the course of the text, including its relationship to the characters, setting, and plot; provide an objective summary of the text.

◆ CCSS.ELA-LITERACY.RL.8.3: Analyze how particular lines of dialogue or incidents in a story or drama propel the action, reveal aspects of a character, or provoke a decision.

◆ CCSS.ELA-LITERACY.W.8.9: Draw evidence from literary or informational texts to support analysis, reflection, and research.

Day Twelve: Reflecting on our Text Sets

Before Class:
◆ Finish book-length text.
◆ Bring all three works in your text set to class.
◆ Complete the graphic organizer on key text themes started on Day Eleven if you weren't able to finish it in class.

Key Learning Activities:
◆ Mini-lesson: Reflecting on important insights and concepts in our text sets. Sean conducts a mini-lesson that focuses on reflecting on how individual works can combine to build overarching understandings of essential questions. Building on the previous day's discussion of key themes, this lesson addresses how different texts can combine to contribute to understandings of key concepts.

◆ Model activity: Sean models what it looks like to reflect on important insights and concepts in text sets. To do this, he completes a graphic organizer on which he writes his essential question, the titles of each of the texts in his text set, and an explanation of how each text has informed his understanding of the essential question.

◆ Follow-up: Students work on the activity Sean modeled, using the same graphic organizer. They use the organizer to reflect on how each text in their text sets has informed their understandings of the essential question in their units. Since this is an important activity that can inform students' final assessments, they spend the majority of class time working on it. Sean confers with students while they work, asking them clarifying questions and helping them create in-depth responses.

◆ Small-group activity: Students share their graphic organizers with their group members. Group members talk to each other about what reflections are most clear and which ones can benefit from additional detail.

◆ Individual follow-up: Students return to their graphic organizers, looking for any reflections or ideas on it that can benefit from additional detail. Sean checks in with students as they do this.

◆ Exit question: What is one way that a work in your text set has informed your understanding of your essential question?

Key Standards Addressed:

◆ VA SOL 8.5: The student will read and analyze a variety of fictional texts, literary nonfiction, poetry, and drama.

◆ VA SOL 8.7: The student will write in a variety of forms to include narrative, expository, persuasive, and reflective with an emphasis on expository and persuasive writing.

◆ CCSS.ELA-LITERACY.RL.8.1: Cite the textual evidence that most strongly supports an analysis of what the text says explicitly as well as inferences drawn from the text.

◆ CCSS.ELA-LITERACY.RL.8.2: Determine a theme or central idea of a text and analyze its development over the course of the text, including its relationship to the characters, setting, and plot; provide an objective summary of the text.

◆ CCSS.ELA-LITERACY.RL.8.3: Analyze how particular lines of dialogue or incidents in a story or drama propel the action, reveal aspects of a character, or provoke a decision.

◆ CCSS.ELA-LITERACY.W.8.9: Draw evidence from literary or informational texts to support analysis, reflection, and research.

Day Thirteen: Final Assessment Work Session

Before Class:

- ◆ Work on final unit assessment. Bring Day Twelve's graphic organizer as well as all notes, drafts, outlines, ideas, and materials to class.

Key Learning Activities:

- ◆ Review of guidelines and rubric for final unit assessment.
- ◆ In-class work time on assessment.
- ◆ One-on-one conferences with teacher.
- ◆ Opportunities for peer feedback.
- ◆ Exit question: Describe the progress you made today on your assessment.

Key Standards Addressed:

- ◆ VA SOL 8.7: The student will write in a variety of forms to include narrative, expository, persuasive, and reflective with an emphasis on expository and persuasive writing.
- ◆ CCSS.ELA-LITERACY.W.8.1.B: Support claim(s) with logical reasoning and relevant evidence, using accurate, credible sources and demonstrating an understanding of the topic or text.
- ◆ CCSS.ELA-LITERACY.W.8.4: Produce clear and coherent writing in which the development, organization, and style are appropriate to task, purpose, and audience.
- ◆ CCSS.ELA-LITERACY.W.8.9: Draw evidence from literary or informational texts to support analysis, reflection, and research.

A note about this class meeting: If you want more time to confer with students, feel like they could benefit from extra in-class work time, or both, you may want to repeat this session to ensure students have the amount of support and time they need to successfully complete their assessments.

Day Fourteen: Final Assessment Publishing Celebration

Before Class:
- ◆ Complete final unit assessment. Bring a hard copy of your assessment for our publishing celebration and to turn in.

Key Learning Activities:
- ◆ Students share verbal summaries of the insights they shared in their assessments and the texts they selected.
- ◆ Assessment publishing celebration, in which students read one another's works and write positive comments on an attached sheet at the end of the piece.
- ◆ Exit question: What is something you read in a peer's assessment that impressed you?

Key Standards Addressed:
- ◆ VA SOL 8.7: The student will write in a variety of forms to include narrative, expository, persuasive, and reflective with an emphasis on expository and persuasive writing.
- ◆ CCSS.ELA-LITERACY.W.8.1.B: Support claim(s) with logical reasoning and relevant evidence, using accurate, credible sources and demonstrating an understanding of the topic or text.
- ◆ CCSS.ELA-LITERACY.W.8.4: Produce clear and coherent writing in which the development, organization, and style are appropriate to task, purpose, and audience.
- ◆ CCSS.ELA-LITERACY.W.8.9: Draw evidence from literary or informational texts to support analysis, reflection, and research.

Key Takeaway Ideas

- ◆ The objective of this chapter is to describe inquiry-based literature instruction that supports students as they design their own inquiry focuses, essential questions, and text sets.
- ◆ By providing students with opportunities to study issues, questions, and texts that especially matter to them, we can further enhance their feelings of agency, power, and freedom in their study of literature.

Overview Suggestions for Putting This Unit Into Action

- ◆ The unit described in this chapter is a progression from the inquiry-based units detailed in Chapters Three and Four. We recommend implementing these three unit structures in sequence in order to maximize students' experiences with the possibilities and affordances of inquiry-based literature instruction.

◆ As they progress through these units, students can feel increasingly comfortable and familiar with inquiry-based literature instruction and the features of essential questions and varied text sets that draw on a number of genres.

◆ While your students navigate the process of constructing and engaging in their own inquiries, we recommend doing the same along with them. When Sean did this along with his students, he found that the practice allowed him to model and explain important activities and processes throughout the unit.

◆ When teaching this unit to his students, Sean asked his students to read their book-length texts nightly for homework and during a designated independent reading time in each day's class. These different reading opportunities helped students manage their amount of reading they needed to complete for their units. When working with your students, we recommend giving them a number of opportunities to read in class to help them complete the reading. Also, at the beginning of the unit, we recommend clearly conveying the unit's time frame so that students can reflect on texts they believe they complete during that time.

Specific Tips for Guiding Students Through This Unit

◆ When you introduce this type of unit to your students, we recommend having a conversation with them that conveys how it is similar to and different from other inquiry-based units they've experienced.

◆ We also suggest emphasizing to students that the processes in which they engage in this unit exemplify the problem-solving scenarios frequently found in real-life, authentic situations. In life, individuals have questions and need to find texts to answer those questions. This unit engages students in that authentic process.

◆ One of the first parts of engaging students in this unit is helping them brainstorm big-picture topics that interest them. To help them do this, we recommend modeling the process for them by listing overarching issues and topics that matter to you and that you would like to explore further. This gives students insight into what the brainstorming process can look like, which can inform their work as they do this on their own.

◆ After students have brainstormed big-picture topics, the next step is for them to choose a topic and create an essential question that extends from that topic. We recommend helping students do this by talking with them about key attributes of essential questions and modeling for them how you turn a big-picture topic that interests you into an essential question.

- ◆ Once students have identified essential questions that will drive their inquiries, they're ready to move to the next step of designing their own inquiry-based units: selecting the texts they'll use to answer their essential questions. One of the first steps of helping students with this selection process is to communicate the parameters of their selections. For example, when Sean conducted this unit with his eighth-graders, he asked them to select one book-length work and two texts from the genres of poetry, art, music, film, television, or another approved option.

Resources and Reminders

- ◆ As with the units described in Chapters Three and Four, we recommend creating a unit rationale that you'll share with administrators, parents, and students to convey key features of the unit and orient all parties involved to its goals, procedures, benefits, and expectations. You can use this rationale to ensure that all of these stakeholders have clear understandings of why you're teaching this unit and what it can do for students' academic and personal needs, emphasizing the agency, ownership, and opportunities for meaningful and academically challenging inquiries that characterize this unit.
- ◆ When creating the unit's assessment, we recommend asking students to analyze and synthesize the works in their text sets to respond to their individually selected essential questions.
- ◆ The graphic organizers used in this unit are available in Appendix B: Unit Planning Templates and Guides.

A Final Insight

- ◆ The unit described in this chapter centers students' curiosities, ideas, and passions. It creates opportunities for students to study issues, questions, and texts that especially matter to them. Based on the student-interest-driven principles of Genius Hour (Krebs & Zvi, 2015), this method of inquiry-based learning is meant to maximize students' opportunities for choice and ownership in a supportive and structured context of inquiry-based learning.

Section Three
Putting It All Together

6

Assessing Inquiry

In a classroom that privileges inquiry, assessment can play an important part in helping teachers and their students know areas of strength and areas of improvement. By its nature, inquiry is not well-aligned to high-stakes exams or standardized tests. The ways in which inquiry allows individual students to read, write, listen, speak, and learn in myriad directions necessitates assessment practices that honor this.

We know that assessment has a crucial place in the English Language Arts classroom in so much as it helps teachers and students know what has been learned and what opportunities for learning are available. Engaging in inquiry work and the assessment of students' inquiries may indeed look a bit different than traditional, end-of-unit assessments that may emphasize a "right" answer or a particular letter on a multiple-choice examination. We know teachers are striving for assessments that are authentic, assessments that provide students opportunities to engage with content in ways that people do outside of the school walls.

We believe that there are grand opportunities to engage in authentic, meaningful assessments within the context of inquiry units. In this chapter, we aim to articulate how assessing inquiry aligns with the ways in which the field, broadly, discusses assessment. Then, we share a few practical, engaging assessments that your students will find meaningful and you will find helpful as you consider what students have learned from engaging in inquiry work.

How Assessing Inquiry Aligns With Contemporary Views on Assessment

Our views on assessment and assessing inquiry, in particular, align well with what key organizations and thinkers in the field have had to say about assessment. The National Council of Teachers of English (2018) writes:

> Literacy assessment is an integral part of literacy teaching and learning; that literacy assessment contributes to the conditions for literacy teaching and learning; and that professional knowledge about literacy assessment is a critical component of a literacy teacher's development and practice.

We encourage teachers to think about what it is they want to learn about their students as they design assessments for inquiry. In this way, assessment is the bridge between teaching and learning (Wiliam, 2013). What we teachers learn from students through assessment informs future instruction: "Assessments should provide additional information and direction for instruction" (Risko & Walker-Dalhouse, 2012, p. 41). In this vein, the assessments we suggest below enable teachers and students to learn more about particular strengths and areas of improvement.

The International Literacy Association's (2017) brief "Literacy Assessment: What Everyone Needs to Know" articulates that "Reading and writing are complex areas to assess. No single assessment can include all aspects of these complex processes" (p. 1). The brief suggests that in the context of high-stakes testing, it can be difficult to use information to inform teaching and learning and that "too often, assessments are chosen for technical measurement properties rather than for the likelihood of productive consequences for students and teachers" (ILA, 2017, p. 6). Our suggestions for assessing inquiry line up with the following assertion:

> All assessments—regardless of purpose—should provide useful and timely information about desired literacy goals. They should be composed of authentic literacy activities as opposed to contrived texts or tasks generated specifically for assessment purposes. The quality of assessment information should not be sacrificed for the efficiency of an assessment procedure.
>
> (ILA, 2017, p. 4)

As such, the assessment recommendations that follow are authentic in that they fit with the purpose of a curriculum dedicated to inquiry-based learning and represent ways in which writers and readers in the real world can share responses to inquiry.

In their book *Be That Teacher!: Breaking the Cycle for Struggling Readers*, Risko and Walker-Dalhouse (2012) assert that assessments should meet the following criteria to be meaningful for instructional planning:

◆ Situated in the students' perspective
◆ Situating in authentic reading activities
◆ Focused on more than single skills and/or strategies simultaneously
◆ Both formative and summative
◆ Multimodal
◆ Doable in the real life classrooms

(p. 39)

Their criteria provide a framework that can be used to analyze how teachers assess inquiry. The nature of inquiry work underscores students' perspectives, as they are creating inquiry questions, selecting texts, and sharing ideas about how the texts inform the inquiry question throughout the inquiry unit. Furthermore, students are given opportunities to engage in authentic reading activities. What is so grand about inquiry work in the literacy classroom is that it mimics what people do in the real world. If someone has a question, they rely on texts to consider possible answers and perspectives. The complex nature of inquiry work necessitates that students are working on multiple skills (e.g., researching, synthesizing, paraphrasing, inferring, comparing and contrasting, etc.) across multiple language domains (i.e., reading, writing, speaking, and listening) at the same time. The informal and formal nature of inquiry assessments makes possible both formative and summative assessment opportunities. Multimodal responses, discussed later, can be wonderful ways for students to share what they have learned and thought about as a result of engaging in an inquiry unit. And, of course, inquiry work and assessing inquiry can indeed be done in the real-life classroom, in part, because inquiry is an authentic literacy practice.

Ideas to Consider When Assessing Inquiry

It is clear that effective assessment measures within the context of an inquiry unit align well with contemporary thoughts about assessment in general. Before we recommend methods for assessing inquiry, we wanted to give teachers a few thinking questions to ask themselves as they consider ways to assess students' inquiry work.

How does my assessment align with the purpose of my inquiry unit? As we have discussed, we do not believe inquiry work fits perfectly with standardized, multiple-choice exams. We encourage teachers to think about the ways in which the assessment they or the students decide upon aligns with the initial goals of the inquiry unit. Returning to the essential questions posed or created by students and thinking through the ways in which the assessment allows students to share their learning in this particular area are helpful starting points.

How am I involving students in assessment? Some teachers have had great success in allowing students to co-create their assessments and their assessment criteria (e.g., rubrics) with teachers. We know how important choice can be for students. Are there particular choices students can have as they select a project that will highlight their learning? In addition to providing students opportunities to select their assessment mode, some teachers allow students to fill in areas of the rubric that are specific to their particular goals. Whether or not a rubric is used, student checklists can be helpful as students progress through an inquiry unit and its assessment. Listing the criteria and giving students the opportunity to check off whether they are at a particular area of completion helps draw students into the process. For example, in the book *Writing Pathways: Performance Assessments and Learning Progressions*, Lucy Calkins (2015) includes student checklists that include the following areas for students to mark next to each assessment area: "not yet," "starting to," and "yes!" Having students assess their progress along the way helps them become more metacognitive. Depending upon the nature of the inquiry assessment, peer review might really help students consider audience but also receive targeted feedback related to specific questions they have about their assessment.

In what ways am I informally assessing students' literacies during the inquiry unit? The importance of informal assessment during an inquiry unit cannot be emphasized enough. Understanding that students' responses to the inquiry question are part of the summative evaluation is just one aspect of assessing students' literacies. Think about the opportunities to assess students' fluency and comprehension by having brief conferences with them during their independent reading time. How might you incorporate mini-lessons to address areas of growth and collect exit slips at the end of independent reading time so as to see how students applied particular reading strategies? How might small writing exercises be incorporated within an inquiry unit to help students develop in particular areas? Understanding the small group and whole class sharing time as a way to assess students' speaking and listening skills can lead to some powerful insights. In some ways, we are advocating for teachers to think of every classroom moment within an inquiry unit as an opportunity to find out more about students. The unit plan descriptions in Chapters Three, Four, and Five feature a variety of informal assessment opportunities, such as daily exit questions, one-on-one conferences during student independent work time, and small-group and whole-class discussions. We encourage you to utilize these informal assessments to monitor student learning during inquiry-based instruction.

How can students apply the work done on the inquiry assessment in future career or academic contexts? In line with the Common Core State Standards and other current state standards, analyzing your assessment in the context of students' future career and academic contexts can be meaningful. Having students complete assessments that may inform what they do in the future can be a motivational factor. Authentic assessments that ask students to think across multiple disciplines, which many of the suggested assessments that follow can do, will only enrich their understanding of a particular inquiry.

What aspects of the assessment project would you find meaningful and motivating if you were the student? This simple question can be quite powerful. Thinking about how you might respond to being assigned a particular assessment is helpful when considering the perspective your students might have on it. This reflective question also helps teachers consider the authenticity aspect of assessments. It helps to think critically about the utility of the assessment beyond just a grade, and doing this often helps us make thoughtful decisions.

Recommended Methods for Assessing Inquiry

Now that we have shared how contemporary thinking about assessment aligns with our vision for assessing inquiry as well as a few reflective questions teachers might ask themselves as they are thinking about assessing inquiry, we move now to methods for assessing inquiry.

Whereas this is certainly not an exhaustive list, it is our hope that the following recommended methods will help your efforts in assessing inquiry. We have tried to incorporate methods that allow students to develop their abilities in reading, writing, listening, and speaking skills; refine their abilities to engage in new literacies practices; and engaging in community-based assessments that allow them to extend their inquiry-learning beyond the classroom.

The recommendations that follow move along a continuum of more traditional assessments that may look and feel like assignments students are already doing in the classroom to assessments that may look and feel less familiar. We anticipate that this continuum will provide teachers with a safe starting point and inspiration to incorporate other assessment methods in the future.

Reflection/Essay

Essays are powerful ways for students to be able to reflect on their learning within the context of an inquiry-based unit. Essays provide students an opportunity to work on traditional writing skills while still engaging in meaningful inquiry work. Reflective essays, like the ones shared in the three units within Chapters Three, Four, and Five, provided students opportunities to demonstrate what they learned about a particular teacher- or self-selected inquiry as they made claims and used textual evidence to do so. As powerful learning exercises, these reflective pieces can help students articulate their own learning. Teachers who are looking to enhance their students' reflective writing may find Fink's (2013) work on reflections helpful. His six categories (i.e., foundational knowledge, application, integration, human dimension, caring, and learning how to learn) can help teachers formulate reflective prompts to best help their students.

Socratic Seminars

As we talked about in Chapter Three, it is important to think about how to help all students develop the four language domains. Whereas it might be most natural to think about reading and writing, it is also important to think about listening and speaking. An assessment we believe plays nicely into this goal is a Socratic Seminar. There are multiple ways we could envision Socratic Seminars taking place with an inquiry unit. Imagine the growth one could see if students were provided an opportunity to have a seminar at the beginning and end of an inquiry unit. We always advocate for preparing students with prompts and time to prepare for seminars before engaging in them. Students who have never participated may need additional scaffolding. Taking a look at example Socratic seminars available online and/or videotaping students engaging in Socratic seminars, with student and parent permission, and then showing these recordings to them can be powerful learning opportunities.

Text-Set Review Blog Post

As we shared in Chapter Five, helping students create text sets that will help them answer particular inquiry questions can be quite successful. To extend this unit idea with an assessment that allows students to engage in new literacies practices, teachers can have students create a book blog post to highlight and review the texts they read for other readers in their class, school, and beyond. Building upon the idea that literacy is a social practice, this assessment allows students to write for an authentic audience of their peers while sharing their thoughts and communicating how each text helped them consider their inquiry. There are a variety of ways teachers could go about assessing inquiry in this manner. Depending upon privacy concerns and challenges, students could type these reviews for others to read as they walk in the hallway; use a classroom-protected space to post reviews, such as Google Classroom; or create blog posts with WordPress or another blog platform.

Podcasts

Another way to engage students with new literacies practices and allow them space to share their new understandings about their particular inquiry is to have them create podcasts. Students could create individual podcasts in which they share what texts they have examined and how these texts helped them gain new knowledge about the inquiry they were investigating. They could also collaborate with classmates to create a podcast that includes an interview format. Students could also interview people outside of their classroom so as to gain perspectives about their inquiry question that may confirm or challenge what they figured out in pursuit of their inquiry. Again, we acknowledge that creating podcasts to publish on the Internet might not be an option in every district. In this case, having students perform their podcasts in front of the class in a sort of in-the-recording-studio format could work really nicely. If podcasting in its most authentic format is a possibility, we have had success with Anchor.

Social Media Account

Creating a class Twitter/Instagram/Tik Tok account around a particular inquiry is another assessment possibility. Asking students to contribute texts, articles, photographs, ideas, and relevant hashtags to a social media account, perhaps one that is shared by the class, could be a valuable way for students to not only demonstrate that their thinking about the inquiry extended beyond the in-class texts they read but also an opportunity to help students understand the power of social media and the ways in which writing for social media differs from writing a traditional print text. We recommend being current with the social media platforms that are popular at the moment.

Gallery

Many of the prior assessment methods ask students to use the texts read and analyzed as part of the inquiry unit and demonstrate how their understanding of the inquiry has expanded. Instead of solely responding to previously-created works, another way to assess students' understandings of the inquiry is to have them create an original piece of art in which they demonstrate understanding, respond to particular texts they explored, or reflect on their inquiry journey in the context of a particular inquiry question. Students could select to write, draw, or perform this for their classmates or a broader audience. The open-endedness of this assessment allows for student choice and allows each student to respond to inquiry in their unique way.

Letter or Email for Change

The nature of inquiry allows students to think about their place in the world and the different perspectives around particular issues and topics. To broaden students' abilities to advocate for change in their communities, having students compose a letter or email for change is another assessment idea. Many teachers who engage in inquiry work want students to connect their in-class text analysis to the world beyond the classroom walls. Allowing students to showcase their new understandings of a particular inquiry, reveal evidence from texts they have examined, and develop their traditional writing skills, a letter or email for change allows students to apply their understandings as they advocate for change in their school, community, or world. This assessment allows teachers and students to meet more traditional writing standards while engaging in authentic literacy practices.

Planning or Assisting With an Event

One of the most powerful aspects of engaging in inquiry work is its application to the real world. Teachers and students are engaging in authentic investigations of topics and issues and questions that matter. Planning an event (e.g., a drive) or assisting with an event (e.g., creating the program for a community organization's event) is an assessment method that can help students understand the relevance of exploring big questions within their communities. Teachers and students may also be on the lookout for school clubs that are taking on issues that may be connected to their inquiry questions. Perhaps this is not the first assessment method you try as you are dipping your feet in the inquiry waters. In time, however, having students create an event based on their inquiry questions or partnering with local organizations that may address similar inquiries can be a really powerful way to help students see the importance of inquiry in the real world.

Final Thoughts on Assessment

As you consider the ways in which you assess students' knowledge of the inquiry-based unit you design, think about the assessment's authenticity. Think about how the assessment you ask your students complete relates to the purposes you have selected for engaging in inquiry work and how the assessment provides an opportunity for students to share their new understandings of a particular inquiry. Return to Risko and Walker-Dalhouse's (2012) criteria for assessment.

What is so exciting about assessing students' inquiry is that meaningful, authentic assessments that honors students' voices and provides them with spaces to engage in literacy practices that mimic what people in the real world do. People in the real world have questions. And they read texts to figure out more. And they often respond to these texts in some sort of way: they may reflect, share this knowledge in personal and professional spaces, use this knowledge to create change in their communities, or apply new understandings in their personal and professional lives. The aforementioned assessment recommendations try to mimic this, while providing opportunities for teachers to help their students continue to develop as literate people.

There are myriad ways to assess students' inquiry. We have provided some recommended assessment methods in this chapter, but we know that new literacy practices will come about and replace our recommendations. We also know that teachers are creative people, and that there are, no doubt, multiple ideas for how to assess inquiry spinning around in their heads right now. Regardless of the method selected, we hope that when assessing inquiry, assessments are selected for the ways in which they allow teachers and students to continue to learn more—about themselves as readers, writers, listeners, and speakers—but, most importantly, as people.

7

Supporting English Language Learners in Inquiry-Based Literature Instruction

With the burgeoning population of English Language Learners (ELLs) in our schools, we have an obligation to think about how best to support these students in our English classrooms (National Council of Teachers of English [NCTE], 2020). We rely on Wright's (2019) definition of an *English Language Learner*: "An English Language Learner (ELL) is a student who is in the process of attaining proficiency in English as a new, additional language" (p. 1). We hope that our approach to supporting ELLs in inquiry-based literature instruction can help change the depiction of ELLs Castañeda, Shen, and Claros-Berlioz (2018) painted:

> In addition to the long journey ELs take to acquire academic English language skills, they are often marginalized in the curriculum and in social interactions with their peers. Within the curriculum, ELs' background experiences are often not valued or incorporated, the different ways the families of ELs interact may not be legitimized, and there is often a disconnect between school and home literacy practices. Moreover, cultural differences can influence the way peers interact socially with ELs in and outside of the classroom.
>
> (p. 20)

Certainly, we know this picture does not capture the experience of every ELL in our classrooms. But what we do know is that an inquiry-driven curriculum can help support ELLs in myriad ways.

In this chapter, we share some ideas about the current context of ELLs in our schools and how our approach is informed by culturally responsive teaching. Then, we offer strategies to help support ELLs in an inquiry unit and recommend professional resources to enhance teachers' professional learning in the area of supporting ELLs in the English classroom.

ELLs in the English Classroom

The National Council of Teachers of English's (NCTE) 2020 *NCTE Position Paper on the Role of English Teachers in Educating English Language Learners (ELLs)* asserted that the population of ELLs in our classrooms continues to grow within all types of schools (i.e., urban, suburban, and rural). Cloud, Lakin, Leininger, and Maxwell (2010) shared a problematic high school graduation rate for ELLs. We acknowledge that ELLs may be in myriad classroom settings (e.g., push-in, push-out, English immersion, and mainstream course integration) in any particular building, but most ELLs students are situated in mainstream classrooms (NCTE, 2020), making it imperative that English teachers think about how to make the curriculum accessible to ELLs. It is important to note that ELLs bring to our classrooms diverse linguistic and cultural backgrounds, and many are not immigrants to the United States but rather individuals who were born in our country (Wright, 2019).

Culturally Responsive Teaching

Our approach to helping support ELLs in inquiry work within the English classroom is informed by culturally responsive teaching as defined by Gay (2002): "Culturally responsive teaching is defined as using the cultural characteristics, experiences, and perspectives of ethnically diverse students as conduits for teaching them more effectively" (p. 106). For Ladson-Billings (1995), culturally relevant pedagogy has three criteria: "an ability to develop students academically, a willingness to nurture and support cultural competence, and the development of a sociopolitical or critical consciousness" (p. 483). And whereas these researchers speak specifically about students from diverse backgrounds, we believe that bringing in all students' cultures and backgrounds to the classroom will help forge a connection between the texts they read and their out-of-school lives and the world around them. Teachers who embody a pedagogical approach that privileges culturally responsive teaching learn about their students' languages and cultures. Acquiring information about the home languages of the students in our class can be a good starting point. In addition, learning about students' cultures, contributions that have been made by students' particular ethnic groups is important, and literacy skills in their home language can also be particularly helpful (Gay, 2002; NCTE, 2020).

We also ascribe to a mindset that honors students' home languages in ways that see them as an asset rather than a deficit (Cloud et al., 2010; Wright, 2019). Lacy (2019) discusses creating an interest inventory for her students to learn about who they are and to consider how to incorporate their interests into the curriculum. She includes questions such as "What do you wonder about?", "What topics/things do you want to read about?", and "List five things you are good at." She then promises to represent each of their interests in the school year's reading. Teachers can also invite students to bring texts they read (e.g., recipes, manuals, video game cheat codes, song lyrics, billboards, etc.) into the classroom or to find texts that relate to classroom reading. Providing opportunities for students to share and bring their out-of-school lives into the classroom will only enrich the classroom community. Inquiry units are also ripe with opportunities to provide learner-centered curricula and communities of learners, two aspects of instruction that help support ELLs (Cloud et al., 2010).

Strategies to Help Support ELLs in an Inquiry Unit

In this section, we offer several strategies aimed at helping English teachers support ELLs in an inquiry unit.

Work With Colleagues to Learn About Students' Literacies

We encourage collaboration with colleagues trained specifically to support ELL students (Cloud et al., 2010; NCTE, 2020). We encourage teachers to work with colleagues to ascertain the literacy skills of the ELLs in their classrooms. The WIDA (2012) standards can help teachers consider where their students are on a continuum that includes the terms entering, emerging, developing, expanding, or bridging on a variety of skills. Individual states and districts may also have information about students' literacy in their home language and English from home language surveys and/or other language assessments (Wright, 2019). It is important, too, to understand that students who are no longer identified as ELLs may still need scaffolds to succeed in the English classroom.

Reflect on Curriculum and Materials

After learning about students' languages and cultures, teachers then can reflect on the curriculum and materials. As Gay (2002) wrote, "Culturally responsive teachers know how to determine the multicultural strengths and weaknesses of curriculum designs and instructional materials and make the changes necessary to improve their overall quality" (p. 108). Think critically about the inquiry question posed in the context of students in your classroom. In line with culturally responsive teaching, this strategy will help you analyze whether or not the question posed will honor your students' languages and cultures. Think about the ways in which the inquiry question allows your students to consider questions that are particularly pertinent in their communities.

An inquiry unit that honors students' language and cultures makes possible Bishop's (1990) idea that texts serve as windows, mirrors, and sliding glass doors for students. Think about the ways in which texts within an inquiry curriculum can provide ways for students to see and step into the worlds of diverse cultures and reflect upon their own identities and to answer questions that are particularly pertinent in their communities. Having students create their own inquiry questions helps students do just this.

Analyze Texts Available

Analyze the texts that you will ask students to use to answer the inquiry question or texts available to students if they are selecting text. In this exercise, teachers examine critically the texts to be taught in an inquiry unit. Answer the following questions as you are analyzing:

- ◆ What texts might I select or recommend for students within an inquiry unit?
- ◆ What languages and cultures are represented?
- ◆ What languages and cultures are not represented?
- ◆ Are texts read in class representative of students' languages and cultures?
- ◆ Are representations of students' languages and cultures empowering?
- ◆ What perspectives are included?
- ◆ What perspective are absent?
- ◆ What genres of texts are used for whole-class readings? For independent reading?
- ◆ Are the print texts selected written in English, students' home languages, or a combination of both?
- ◆ How do the texts offer opportunities for students to answer the inquiry in a way that honors their language and culture?

◆ How do school resources (e.g., the classroom library, the school library, digital devices) provide opportunities for students to answer the inquiry in a way that honors their language and culture?

In addition to these questions, The Annenberg Foundation's *Evaluating Multicultural Literacy Grid* (https://www.learner.org/wp-content/uploads/2019/02/Evaluating-Multicultural-Literature-Chart-s6_evaluating_lit-Teaching-English-Language-Learners-Teaching-Reading-3-5-Workshop.pdf) may be a helpful tool for you and your students to use.

Develop Students' Four Language Domains

We believe in a curriculum that helps ELLs learn both language and content (Wright, 2019). As you move beyond the inquiry question and text selection, you want to think about the activities in which students will engage within the inquiry unit. We recommend thinking about how you are helping your students develop in each of the four language domains: listening, speaking, reading, and writing (Wright, 2019). As Cloud et al. (2010) share, "Without proficiency in all English-language skills—listening, speaking, reading, and writing—students cannot acquire or demonstrate their knowledge of the subject matter taught in middle and high schools" (p. 7). Think about the ways in which you provide opportunities for students to engage in each domain. Though we discuss them separately next, ELLs are best served when they are given opportunities to integrate these four domains (Cloud et al., 2010) throughout an inquiry unit. The following statement from Cloud et al. (2010) illustrates exactly what we think possible in an engaging inquiry-based literature unit:

If we choose themes that engage our learners, they will want to speak and share their thoughts with us. If we motivate learners with engaging reading material, they will want to talk and write about it. We need to engage our learners fully so that they cannot wait to speak and they will want to write. This means selecting topics that promote real dialogue and sharing—high-interest topics that draw even the most reluctant learner into speaking and writing activities.

(p. 83)

Listening and Speaking. There are many ways to help develop ELL students' listening and speaking skills during the course of an inquiry unit. Of course, class discussions around the inquiry question will promote listening and speaking, ensuring that students practice receiving comprehensible input and producing comprehensible output (Wright, 2019). Students may even benefit from having some discussion prompts or sentence starters so as to scaffold their entry into a discussion. Small group discussions may make students feel more comfortable. And if you want to have students engage in a whole-class discussion, consider providing students time to practice their responses with a partner or in a small group. Another strategy that will help students' listening skills is to have students listen to an audio version of the text (Wright, 2019) they are reading as they respond to the inquiry question posed. To build students' speaking skills, encourage them to retell what they have read or give oral presentations (informal or formal) about the content (Wright, 2019). Reading aloud to ELLs (Wright, 2019) in order to model effective fluency will help build students' listening and reading skills, which is the topic of our next section.

Reading. The texts students read in pursuit of the answer to the inquiry posed will help students develop their reading skills. In line with culturally responsive pedagogy, consider whether there are opportunities for your students to read texts in their home languages and whether or not the texts selected by you or the students are relevant to the particular students in the classroom (Cloud et al., 2010). Provide time for students to preview the texts they will be reading during the inquiry unit, and set a purpose for reading texts; anticipation guides and visual graphs to help them track their responses to readings may also scaffold ELL students' reading (Cloud et al., 2010).

Previewing the vocabulary in the texts students may use is also helpful when considering the needs of ELL students. Beck, McKeown, and Kucan (2013) discuss a three-tier word model that is important to consider when words students might encounter as they read. Tier one words are basic (e.g., *dog*) to which students are exposed often. Tier two words (e.g., *precede*) "are of high utility for mature language users and are found across a variety of domains" (p. 9). Students see these words in texts but are less likely to hear them in conversations. Third tier words (e.g., *epidermis*) are domain specific. Beck et al. (2013) recommended instruction on the tier two words. Having students create individualized dictionaries (Wright, 2019) may also support ELL students throughout an inquiry unit.

In their book *Disrupting Thinking: Why How We Read Matters*, Beers and Probst (2017) shared a framework to help readers think deeply about the texts they read. The framework, known as the BHH framework, helps readers consider what is in the book, in their heads, and in their hearts. First, readers want to consider what the book is saying, then how this makes them think differently or similarly than before, and, finally, what they learned about themselves and the broader world. We believe the last two elements are particularly relevant to helping students make real-world connections, exactly what we hope to have them do in inquiry-based literature instruction. Of course, we believe that allowing students to select their own texts helps build motivation around reading and enhances reading abilities (Wright, 2019).

Graphic organizers may also help ELLs comprehend texts and provide students support when discussing their reading (Wright, 2019). Inviting ELL students to engage in reader's theater in which they make up their own scripts after reading a text is also another way to help students develop their comprehension and build language skills (Wright, 2019). If possible, consider using digital texts that offer students additional experiences (e.g., audio recordings, videos, bilingual elements, definitions, etc.) to help their understanding of texts (Wright, 2019).

Writing. There are a variety of ways in which writing can be incorporated in inquiry units. Many researchers (Cloud et al., 2010; Fu, 2009; Wright, 2019) have discussed the importance of having students write in their primary language. Acknowledging the power in welcoming students to speak and write in their home languages is a helpful perspective to take.

Other writing techniques may include modeled writing (when you write and the students watch), shared writing (when you write based on students' comments), guided writing (when you provide a mini-lesson and then students write), and interactive writing (when students write but you think together). These practices can be helpful in helping to meet ELLs where they are as writers (Wright, 2019). Journaling can also be a way to improve ELL students' writing (Wright, 2019), and asking students to return to their journals as they progress through an inquiry will help them work on writing skills and continue to adjust their thinking about their responses to the inquiry. As students progress through an inquiry unit, word walls and thematic word charts may help them incorporate particular terms into their writing (Wright, 2019). Whenever possible, consider helping students learn cognates (Cloud et al., 2010). Consider taking students through the process of writing workshop (Atwell, 2014; Wright, 2019) as students produce more formal texts in response to an inquiry question. We discussed how to incorporate all students' identities into the writing they do within inquiry units as part of our previous assessment chapter.

Engage Students in Authentic Experiences to Solve Real-World Problems

Having students engage in authentic experiences after they read texts will only make more real the connections between the texts they read and their out-of-school lives and the world around them. Lewison, Flint, and Van Sluys's (2002) ideas about critical literacy (disrupting the commonplace, interrogating multiple perspectives, focusing on sociopolitical issues, and taking action and promoting justice) fit in well with this approach. In response to a particular inquiry, have students create a project (e.g., a poem, a book, a blog post, a letter, a service-learning project, a food drive, an exhibit in the school library, a series of social media posts, a song, etc.). This will allow them to contribute to the betterment of their school or community—and will help them understand that the true beauty of a text is not necessarily within its words, sounds, or colors but in its ability to evoke thought and change. Reading about particular issues in one community might help students consider how that issue or a similar one is affecting community members:

> Diverse literature can transform students' identities and the narratives they carry about the people they encounter. It can support students' reading and writing development. When reading diverse literature, students can communicate critically about issues important to their communities and the world at large.
>
> (ILA, 2018)

We believe that if students are asked to make connections between the texts and their community and then are provided an opportunity to enact some social change in their community English teachers will be able to not only bolster students' motivation to read but community engagement in the present and in the future. More information on how to engage students in authentic experiences to solve real-world problems is included in our assessment chapter.

Recommended Professional Resources

Here, we recommend several professional resources that may be helpful as you think about doing inquiry work with ELLs in mind.

Colorin' Colorado
(www.colorincolorado.org/) This bilingual website provides help for families and teachers as they support ELLs.

Edutopia's Resources for Teaching English Language Learners
(https://www.edutopia.org/article/resources-for-teaching-english-language-learners-ashley-cronin) This page helps teachers consider how to help ELLs in a variety of ways and is organized using the following headers: General Tips and Strategies, Boosting Student Engagement, Language and Literacy Instruction, Learning English Through the Arts, and Using Technology with ELLs.

Jennifer Gonzales's "12 Ways to Support English Learners in the Mainstream Classroom" Cult of Pedagogy Podcast
(www.cultofpedagogy.com/supporting-esl-students-mainstream-classroom/) This podcast provides teachers with ideas about how to support ELLs.

Teaching Channel's Teacher Toolkit: English Language Learners

(https://www.teachingchannel.com/blog/teacher-toolkit-ell) This website includes articles under the following headers: Best Practices, Lesson Ideas and Strategies, and Planning.

TESOL

(www.tesol.org/) This website of the Teaching English to Speakers of Other Languages organization provides resources and professional development opportunities for teachers.

We Need Diverse Books

(https://diversebooks.org/) We Need Diverse Books is a nonprofit organization that aims to ensure that books published represent young people. The organization has a website as well as social media sites and has published three anthologies: *Flying Lessons & Other Stories*, *Fresh Ink*, and *The Hero Next Door*.

WIDA Standards

(https://wida.wisc.edu/sites/default/files/resource/2012-ELD-Standards.pdf) These standards help teachers learn how to support ELLs. The Can Do Philosophy takes a positive perspective on ELL, and the standards provide multiple ways for teachers to assess an ELL's progress.

SIOP

(www.cal.org/siop/products/) The Sheltered Instruction Observation Protocol (SIOP) can be a valuable tool for individual students and schools to use as they evaluate the way they support ELLs.

8

Key Recommendations to Keep in Mind When Conducting Inquiry-Driven Units

Now that you've read the first seven chapters of this book, you've developed important understandings of inquiry-based literature instruction. You've explored what this form of instruction is, why it has the potential to make such a significant impact on students, the role of essential questions in conducting effective inquiries, and a variety of ways inquiry-based literature instruction can look in practice. In this final chapter, we share five key recommendations to keep in mind when putting the ideas in this book into action by conducting inquiry-driven literature units in your own classroom:

- ◆ Center students in inquiry-based instruction by incorporating their interests and curiosities.
- ◆ Reflect on the components of high-quality essential questions.
- ◆ Construct inquiry-driven units that incorporate a wide range of texts.
- ◆ Gradually release additional responsibility to students over multiple inquiry-driven units.
- ◆ Create opportunities for students to demonstrate the results of their inquiries in meaningful ways.

These statements synthesize key ideas discussed in this text, providing some important takeaway points for you to reflect on as you think about implementing inquiry-based literature instruction in your class. If, while utilizing this instructional approach, you decide that you want a brief overview of key suggestions that will maximize its effectiveness, we recommend revisiting this chapter for highlights of important suggestions. Then, if you feel you want more detail about a specific instructional practice or idea discussed in this book, you can reexamine the chapter in the book specifically dedicated to that concept. (For example, if you read this chapter and want to reflect even more deeply on the features of strong essential questions, you can revisit Chapter Two to do so.) Now, let's consider each of this chapter's five key recommendations in detail.

Recommendation One: Center Students in Inquiry-Based Instruction by Incorporating Their Interests and Curiosities

One of the most important and useful features of inquiry-based literature instruction is that it creates natural opportunities for students to investigate topics that truly matter to them. Inquiry-based teaching and learning provides students with authentic experiences: this instructional approach mirrors what people do in their lives when they have questions about topics that matter to them. In these situations, individuals reflect on concepts that they want to understand further, delve into information about those concepts, and generate conclusions based on the sources they examined and their analyses of those sources. Through inquiry-based learning, students can have these same authentic, interest-based experiences that prioritize their interests.

Whether you as the teacher are structuring the focus of the unit or students are selecting their own topics, there are many ways to connect inquiry-based learning to students' interests. For example, in the units described in Chapters Three and Four in which Sean identified the focal topics and essential questions for the units in which he and his students engaged, he identified issues that were of high-interest to his students and lent themselves to strong inquiries and used these as the starting points for the inquiries in which the class engage. Of course, the unit format discussed in Chapter Five of this book in which students select their own inquiry topics lends itself directly to students' interests, as it asks students to identify concepts that matter to them and use those to construct their own inquiries. By incorporating students' interests in the unit creation process, each of these examples of inquiry-based literature instruction centered students by prioritizing issues and topics that mattered to them. To maximize the effectiveness of your own inquiry-based instruction, we encourage you to do this as well. Talk to your students about issues, ideas, and topics that interest them and spark their curiosities. Listen to what they talk about in class during both structured and unstructured time, such as their concerns and questions about the world. Use what students have to say to construct inquiry-based learning experiences that center their thoughts, questions, and ideas.

Recommendation Two: Reflect on the Components of High-Quality Essential Questions

An integral aspect of strong inquiry-based instruction is an essential question that drives that inquiry in a meaningful way. As Sean explained to his students when introducing inquiry-based learning to them, "Inquiry is all about answering a question. If you have a strong and interesting question, you'll have a strong and meaningful inquiry." In Chapter Two of this book, we discuss key scholarly insights about the features of strong essential questions, such as the seven characteristics of essential questions identified by McTighe and Wiggins (2013):

- ◆ is open-ended;
- ◆ is thought-provoking;
- ◆ calls for higher-order thinking;
- ◆ points toward important, transferable ideas;
- ◆ raises additional questions and sparks further inquiry;
- ◆ requires support and justification, not just an answer;
- ◆ and recurs over time, or can be revisited frequently.

(p. 3)

As you think about the essential questions that guide your students' inquiries, we recommend keeping these attributes in mind. For example, when you draft an essential question to use for an inquiry-based unit, you can look back at the McTighe and Wiggins (2013) characteristics and check to see if the question aligns with most or all of the attributes they identify. Similarly, you can use these essential question attributes if you engage your students in a self-selected inquiry unit (like the one described in Chapter Five) in which they create their own essential questions. Talking with students about these characteristics will give them concrete guidelines to keep in mind as they develop their own questions. Whether you create the essential question for the class to investigate or students design their own, a strong essential question is so important to an effective inquiry: thought-provoking, open-ended questions that call for higher-order thinking and require analysis, support, and justification will help students achieve the maximum benefits of inquiry-based learning.

Recommendation Three: Construct Inquiry-Driven Units That Incorporate a Wide Range of Texts

An outstanding feature of inquiry-based literature instruction is that it naturally aligns with the study of a wide range of texts at one time. To capitalize on this benefit, we recommend creating inquiry units that utilize a variety of works addressing the essential question. By doing so, we teachers allow our students to look at thought-provoking essential questions from a range of perspectives. Incorporating this variety of viewpoints can help students approach essential questions with the higher-order thinking skills and thoughtful analysis with which those questions are aligned (McTighe & Wiggins, 2013). If we taught inquiry-based units with just a single text, students would not be able to reflect on and learn from the range of viewpoints that a multi-textual unit facilitates.

When deciding on the texts to incorporate in your inquiry-driven units, we suggest including texts that represent not only a range of perspectives, but also a variety of genres. By sharing with your students works that align with your essential question and contain this array of ideas and forms, you'll convey to them that the question guiding the unit is one that is not limited to a single work or type of work, emphasizing the importance of considering thought-provoking questions in a range of ways. For example, the units described in Chapters Three, Four, and Five require students to consider essential questions through their analyses of texts from a range of genres and creators (such as authors, songwriters, visual artists, and others aligned with particular genres). Chapter Three, for instance, asked for students to use one novel, four songs or song excerpts, three poems, three pieces of visual art, and two nonfiction articles to reflect on and analyze the unit's essential question. The units discussed in Chapters Four and Five utilized fewer texts, but still incorporated a range of works from different genres aligned with their respective essential questions.

When selecting texts for an inquiry-based unit, the first step is to think about the essential question and look for a variety of texts that address that question in some way. As you construct this text set, we encourage you think about works from a range of perspectives that align with that question. For instance, when Sean constructed the text set for the unit discussed in Chapter Three, he chose texts that align with the essential question "What inspires individuals to take part in social action?" but featured different approaches to this question and a range of viewpoints from a variety of backgrounds. As you consider this range of perspectives, we also recommend drawing from a number of genres, as this can further expand the text set and convey to students that they can use a wide variety of works to reflect on essential questions. Through this range of texts, students can think deeply and analytically about the unit's inquiry topic, helping them get the maximum benefit from this experience.

Recommendation Four: Gradually Release Additional Responsibility to Students Over Multiple Inquiry-Driven Units

To help students achieve the maximum benefits of inquiry-based literature instruction, we recommend gradually giving them increased responsibility for and ownership of their learning as you engage them in multiple inquiry-driven units. The units described in Chapters Three, Four, and Five in this book provide an example of how this increased student ownership can look, starting with a unit with a class-wide essential question and multiple works read by all students, then moving to a unit that gave students additional flexibility by asking them to select texts aligned with the whole-class essential, and finally discussing a unit in which students selected their topics, formed essential questions, and crafted text sets.

When incorporating inquiry-based literature in your classroom, you can certainly follow the same sequence of units that Sean taught to his students in Chapters Three, Four, and Five, but we also encourage you to utilize your own judgment and reflect on what your students are ready for at that time. For instance, some classes might be ready to move directly through these unit types, but others might benefit from participating in multiple units with teacher-selected text sets (such as the unit discussed in Chapter Three) before moving to an inquiry-based format like the one described in Chapter Four in which students select their own texts aligned with an essential question. Similarly, some classes might benefit from additional experiences with teacher-created essential questions before engaging in the unit format discussed in Chapter Five in which students craft their own essential questions and text sets. We encourage you to monitor your students' comfort with and understandings of the key aspects of inquiry-based literature instruction as you guide them through the unit types discussed in this book and gradually increase their ownership of and responsibility for their learning. Inquiry-based learning aligns very well with the gradual release of responsibility (Pearson & Gallagher, 1983) and creates natural opportunities for us as teachers to give our students meaningful ways to structure their own authentic learning experiences.

Recommendation Five: Create Opportunities for Students to Demonstrate the Results of Their Inquiries in Meaningful Ways

Another outstanding aspect of inquiry-based literature instruction is that it aligns very well with authentic assessments that allow students to convey their findings in meaningful ways. Since inquiry facilitates the use of a wide range of texts to answer thought-provoking and relevant questions, it follows naturally that the best ways to convey the results of students' inquiries are through assessment forms that ask students to utilize higher-order thinking skills through in-depth synthesis and application of the questions they investigated. Chapter Six of this book, "Assessing Inquiry," discusses a variety of assessment practices to use in inquiry-based literature instruction in order to create opportunities for students to demonstrate the results of their inquiries in authentic and meaningful ways, such as reflections/essays, Socratic Seminars, text-set review blog posts, podcasts, social media accounts, galleries, letters or emails for change, and planning for or assisting with events. All of these forms of assessment provide students with opportunities to engage in thoughtful analysis and application of the ideas and insights they explored in their inquiries. When you reflect on these forms of assessment and consider which ones to use in your classroom, we encourage you to think about how each aligns or relates to the purpose of the inquiry in which students are engaging and how it provides students with opportunities to share the insights they've gained from that inquiry. By ensuring this alignment, you can make sure that the assessments in which students are engaging are meaningful and authentic, which is consistent with the purpose and values of inquiry-based instruction.

A Final Thought

We would like to close this book with a comment that one of Sean's eighth-graders shared with him after engaging in all three of the inquiry-based units described in this book: "This was harder than what we've done before in ELA class, but also way more interesting. I say harder because it made me think a lot more, like about all the texts that are part of the inquiry, how they relate to each other, and how they relate to the essential question. But I also say more interesting because I got to think about things that really matter. The questions were interesting and relatable." This statement reflects the ideal student experience with inquiry-based literature instruction: it should be challenging to students by engaging them in complex learning experiences centered around thought-provoking essential questions, but it should also be engaging and relevant. The ideas, examples, and recommendations described in this book will help you put inquiry-based literature instruction into action in your classroom and will guide you as you give your students challenging and meaningful learning experiences.

Section Four

Resources

Appendix A
Guide for Book Studies

There are many examples of professional book studies that occur as a result of teachers' own inquiries, an instructional coaching component, or a professional development plan. Both Sean and Katie love engaging in professional book studies. There is really no substitute for reading the same book as a colleague or a group of colleagues and then discussing it either in face-to-face or virtual settings. We also acknowledge that book studies can be an individual endeavor as well.

In this appendix, we want to provide you a guide to help you engage with, reflect on, and discuss the chapters in the book. You will find questions catered to each of the chapters in the book. You can examine the questions as you progress through the book or wait until you have finished the book in order to examine these questions.

So brew up a cup of coffee or tea, and start reflecting and discussing!

Section One: Key Background and Context

Introduction: What Is Inquiry-Based Literature Instruction?
1. What three adjectives describe your literature instruction now?
2. What motivated you to read about inquiry-based literature instruction?
3. What are some features of an inquiry-based literature instruction unit?
4. What do you hope to learn from reading this book?

Chapter One: The Importance of Inquiry

1. Why is inquiry important in the literacy classroom?
2. How might you reconsider the nature of the units in your curriculum?
3. What does inquiry-based literature instruction afford teachers and students?
4. What can you apply from this chapter to your classroom?

Chapter Two: Inquiry and Essential Questions

1. How do you currently use essential questions in your planning?
2. In what ways does this chapter allow your understanding of essential questions to develop?
3. What are the advantages of creating essential questions in the literacy classroom?
4. What are some essential questions you would like to have your students explore?
5. What texts might help students explore these essential questions?
6. What can you apply from this chapter to your classroom?

Section Two: What Can Inquiry-Based Literature Instruction Look Like?

Chapter Three: An Inquiry-Driven Unit on Social Action

1. What are the major components of the inquiry-driven unit shared in this chapter?
2. In what ways do standards align with the inquiry-driven unit shared in this chapter?
3. Why is it important to offer a rationale to students and parents?
4. In what ways do texts other than the central text help students answer the essential question in the inquiry-driven unit shared in this chapter?
5. What is the teacher's role in the inquiry-driven unit shared in this chapter?
6. What are the students' roles in the inquiry-driven unit shared in this chapter?
7. How are students assessed in the inquiry-driven unit shared in this chapter?
8. What can you apply from this chapter to your classroom?

Chapter Four: Student-Selected Text Sets in an Inquiry-Driven Unit

1. What are the major components of the inquiry-driven unit shared in this chapter?
2. In what ways do standards align with the inquiry-driven unit shared in this chapter?
3. Why is it important to offer a rationale to students and parents?
4. In what ways do texts other than the central text help students answer the essential question in the inquiry-driven unit shared in this chapter?
5. What is the teacher's role in the inquiry-driven unit shared in this chapter? How is the teacher's role different than in the previous inquiry-driven unit shared?
6. What are the students' roles in the inquiry-driven unit shared in this chapter? How are the students' roles different than in the previous inquiry-driven unit shared?
7. How are students assessed in the inquiry-driven unit shared in this chapter?
8. What can you apply from this chapter to your classroom?

Chapter Five: Connecting Genius Hour and Inquiry Through Student-Selected Inquiries

1. What were the major components of the inquiry-driven unit shared in this chapter?
2. In what ways do standards align with the inquiry-driven unit shared in this chapter?
3. Why is it important to offer a rationale to students and parents?
4. In what ways do texts other than the central text help students answer the essential question in the inquiry-driven unit shared in this chapter?
5. What was the teacher's role in the inquiry-driven unit shared in this chapter? How is the teacher's role different than in the previous inquiry-driven units shared?
6. What were the students' roles in the inquiry-driven unit shared in this chapter? How are students' roles different than in the previous inquiry-driven units shared?
7. How are students assessed in the inquiry-driven unit shared in this chapter?
8. What can you apply from this chapter to your classroom?

Section Three: Putting It All Together

Chapter Six: Assessing Inquiry

1. How would you describe your approach to assessment in your classroom?
2. How does assessing inquiry as described in the chapter align with contemporary views on assessment?
3. How might you incorporate the ways you currently assess your students' literacies into your inquiry-driven units?
4. What can you apply from this chapter to your classroom?

Chapter Seven: Supporting English Language Learners in Inquiry-Based Literature Instruction

1. How do you support ELLs in your classroom?
2. How might you support ELLs in an inquiry-driven unit?
3. Which of the recommended resources might help you support an ELL's progress through an inquiry-driven unit?
4. What can you apply from this chapter to your classroom?

Chapter Eight: Key Recommendations to Keep in Mind When Conducting Inquiry-Driven Units

1. Reflect back on the three adjectives you used to describe your literacy instruction at the very beginning of this book study. What three adjectives might describe your literacy instruction if you incorporate inquiry-driven units?
2. In what ways will inquiry-driven units help support your students?
3. Which of the five recommendations shared in this chapter do you find most relevant to your literacy instruction?
4. Now that you have finished this book on inquiry-driven units, write down (and share with colleagues, if possible) possible essential questions and texts that you might use to develop an inquiry-driven unit for your students.

Appendix B
Unit Planning Templates and Guides

This appendix is designed to provide you with user-friendly resources that you can use to plan your own inquiry-based units with your students. It contains sections devoted to each unit format described in this book: Unit One—in which the teacher selects the essential question and text set (discussed in Chapter Three); Unit Two—in which the teacher creates an essential question and decides on a read-aloud text for the students (described in Chapter Four); and Unit Three—in which the teacher guides students as they select their own essential question and text sets (detailed in Chapter Five). The unit-specific resources provided here will support you as you plan for teaching these units to your students.

Each unit's section contains a unit planning template that asks you for information relevant to that unit as well as spaces for daily plans. (While the daily plan spaces in these sections each contain 15 plans, you can adapt the number to your needs.) In addition, this appendix contains the graphic organizers Sean used in the student-selected inquiry unit to help students organize their thoughts related to important issues and topics in their units. Our objective in providing these materials is to help guide you as you organize and enact inquiry-based literature instruction in your class. While you can certainly make individual adjustments to your individual planning to align the content and structure of your units with your individual students, these materials can give you a strong planning framework. (These resources are also available on the book's website at www.routledge.com/9780367569358).

 # Unit One: Planning Resources

Essential Question

Why You Chose That Essential Question

Texts Used in the Unit

Text Categories	Text Titles

The Unit Rationale

This unit rationale is divided into four sections: 1) the unit's focus, 2) the unit's key attributes, 3) the unit's connection to educational objectives, and 4) the unit's relevance to students' needs. In each section, record the relevant information to convey the features and benefits of your unit.

The Unit's Focus

The Unit's Key Attributes

The Unit's Connection to Educational Objectives

The Unit's Relevance to Students' Needs

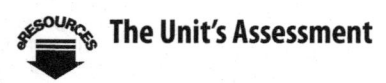

The Unit's Assessment

Assessment Description

Assessment Rubric

Criteria	1	2	3	4	Feedback

1-criteria not met;   2-criteria partially met;   3-criteria met;   4-criteria exceeded

Total score:
Overall feedback:

Outlines of Daily Lesson Plans Used in the Unit

Day One:

Key Learning Activities:

Key Standards Addressed:

Day Two:

Key Learning Activities:

Key Standards Addressed:

Day Three:

Key Learning Activities:

Key Standards Addressed:

Day Four:

Key Learning Activities:

Key Standards Addressed:

Day Five:

Key Learning Activities:

Key Standards Addressed:

Day Six:

Key Learning Activities

Key Standards Addressed:

Day Seven:

Key Learning Activities:

Key Standards Addressed:

Day Eight:

Key Learning Activities:

Key Standards Addressed:

Day Nine:

Key Learning Activities:

Key Standards Addressed:

Day Ten:

Key Learning Activities:

Key Standards Addressed:

Day Eleven:

Key Learning Activities:

Key Standards Addressed:

Day Twelve:

Key Learning Activities:

Key Standards Addressed:

Day Thirteen:

Key Learning Activities:

Key Standards Addressed:

Day Fourteen:

Key Learning Activities:

Key Standards Addressed:

Day Fifteen:

Key Learning Activities:

Key Standards Addressed:

Unit Two: Planning Resources

Essential Question

Why You Chose That Essential Question

The Unit's Read-Aloud Text

How That Read-Aloud Text Aligns With the Essential Question

The Unit Rationale

This unit rationale is divided into four sections: 1) the unit's focus, 2) the unit's key attributes, 3) the unit's connection to educational objectives, and 4) the unit's relevance to students' needs. In each section, record the relevant information to convey the features and benefits of your unit.

The Unit's Focus

The Unit's Key Attributes

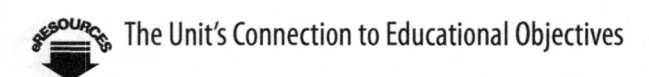

The Unit's Connection to Educational Objectives

The Unit's Relevance to Students' Needs

The Unit's Assessment

Assessment Description

Assessment Rubric

Criteria	1	2	3	4	Feedback

1-criteria not met;   2-criteria partially met;   3-criteria met;   4-criteria exceeded

Total score:
Overall feedback:

Outlines of Daily Lesson Plans Used in the Unit

Day One:

Key Learning Activities:

Key Standards Addressed:

Day Two:

Key Learning Activities:

Key Standards Addressed:

Day Three:

Key Learning Activities:

Key Standards Addressed:

Day Four:

Key Learning Activities:

Key Standards Addressed:

Day Five:

Key Learning Activities:

Key Standards Addressed:

Day Six:

Key Learning Activities:

Key Standards Addressed:

Day Seven:

Key Learning Activities:

Key Standards Addressed:

Day Eight:

Key Learning Activities:

Key Standards Addressed:

Day Nine:

Key Learning Activities:

Key Standards Addressed:

Day Ten:

Key Learning Activities:

Key Standards Addressed:

Day Eleven:

Key Learning Activities:

Key Standards Addressed:

Day Twelve:

Key Learning Activities:

Key Standards Addressed:

Day Thirteen:

Key Learning Activities:

Key Standards Addressed:

Day Fourteen:

Key Learning Activities:

Key Standards Addressed:

Day Fifteen:

Key Learning Activities:

Key Standards Addressed:

Unit Three: Planning Resources

Big-Picture Topics That Interest You (That You Might Model for Your Students)

Essential Question Related to One of Those Big-Picture Topics

Why That Essential Question Interests You

Three Texts Connected to That Essential Question (One Book-Length Text and Two From Other Genres)

Your Thoughts on How Each of Those Texts Aligns With the Essential Question

The Unit Rationale

This unit rationale is divided into four sections: 1) the unit's focus, 2) the unit's key attributes, 3) the unit's connection to educational objectives, and 4) the unit's relevance to students' needs. In each section, record the relevant information to convey the features and benefits of your unit.

The Unit's Focus

The Unit's Key Attributes

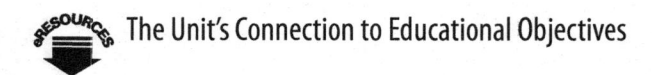

The Unit's Connection to Educational Objectives

The Unit's Relevance to Students' Needs

The Unit's Assessment

Assessment Description

Assessment Rubric

Criteria	1	2	3	4	Feedback

1-criteria not met; 2-criteria partially met; 3-criteria met; 4-criteria exceeded

Total score:

Overall feedback:

Outlines of Daily Lesson Plans Used in the Unit

Day One:

Key Learning Activities:

Key Standards Addressed:

Day Two:

Key Learning Activities:

Key Standards Addressed:

Day Three:

Key Learning Activities:

Key Standards Addressed:

Day Four:

Key Learning Activities:

Key Standards Addressed:

Day Five:

Key Learning Activities:

Key Standards Addressed:

Day Six:

Key Learning Activities:

Key Standards Addressed:

Day Seven:

Key Learning Activities:

Key Standards Addressed:

Day Eight:

Key Learning Activities:

Key Standards Addressed:

Day Nine:

Key Learning Activities:

Key Standards Addressed:

Day Ten:

Key Learning Activities:

Key Standards Addressed:

Day Eleven:

Key Learning Activities:

Key Standards Addressed:

Day Twelve:

Key Learning Activities:

Key Standards Addressed:

Day Thirteen:

Key Learning Activities:

Key Standards Addressed:

Day Fourteen:

Key Learning Activities:

Key Standards Addressed:

Day Fifteen:

Key Learning Activities:

Key Standards Addressed:

Graphic Organizers Used in Student-Selected Inquiry Unit

Graphic Organizer One: Text-Set Brainstorm

Your Essential Question

Books related to the question	Texts of a different genre related to the question	Texts of another genre related to the question

Graphic Organizer Two: How Texts Inform Our Understandings of Essential Questions

Your Essential Question

A text in your text set:	A second text in your text set:	A third text in your text set:
How that text has informed your understanding of your essential question so far:	How that text has informed your understanding of your essential question so far:	How that text has informed your understanding of your essential question so far:

Graphic Organizer Three: Textual Excerpts That Connect to Essential Questions

Your Essential Question

A text in your text set:	A second text in your text set:	A third text in your text set:
A line from that text:	A line from that text:	A line from that text:
How that line connects to your essential question:	How that line connects to your essential question:	How that line connects to your essential question:

Graphic Organizer Four: Distinctions in Ways Texts Address Essential Questions

Your Essential Question

A text in your text set:	A second text in your text set:	A third text in your text set:
Ways the text addresses the essential question (focus on specific ways that are unique to this text):	Ways the text addresses the essential question (focus on specific ways that are unique this text):	Ways the text addresses the essential question (focus on specific ways that are unique to this text):

Graphic Organizer Five: What Has Surprised Us in Our Inquiries

Your Essential Question

Something that has surprised you in your inquiry:	Why it has stood out to you:	How it can inform your response to your essential question:

Graphic Organizer Six: Key Themes and Related Information

Your Essential Question

A key theme you've noticed:	A second key theme you've noticed:	A third key theme you've noticed:
Information related to this theme:	Information related to this theme:	Information related to this theme:

Graphic Organizer Seven: How Our Text Sets Have Informed Our Understandings

Your Essential Question

A text in your text set:	A second text in your text set:	A third text in your text set:
How that text has informed your understanding of your essential question:	How that text has informed your understanding of your essential question:	How that text has informed your understanding of your essential question:

References

Atwell, N. (2014). *In the middle: A lifetime of learning about writing, reading, and adolescents* (3rd ed.). Portsmouth, NH: Heinemann.

Beck, I.L., McKeown, M.G., & Kucan, L. (2013). *Bringing words to life: Robust vocabulary instruction* (2nd ed.). New York, NY: Guilford Press.

Beers, K., & Probst, B. (2017). *Disrupting thinking: Why how we read matters.* New York, NY: Scholastic.

Bishop, R.S. (1990). Mirrors, windows, and sliding glass doors. *Perspectives: Choosing and Using Books for Classrooms, 6*(3).

Brooks, M.D., & Frankel, K.K. (2019). Authentic choice: A plan for independent reading in a restrictive instructional setting. *Journal of Adolescent & Adult Literacy, 62*(5), 574–577.

Calkins, L. (2015). *Writing pathways: Performance assessments and learning progressions.* Portsmouth, NH: Heinemann.

Cartaya, P. (2017). *The epic fail of Arturo Zamora.* New York, NY: Puffin Books.

Castañeda, M., Shen, X., & Claros-Berlioz, E. (2018). English learners (ELs) have stories to tell: Digital storytelling as a venue to bring justice to life. *English Journal, 107*(6), 20–25.

Cloud, N., Lakin, J., Leininger, E., & Maxwell, L. (2010). *Teaching adolescent English language learners: Essentials strategies for middle and high school.* Philadelphia, PA: Caslon.

Coke, P.K. (2018). Using genius hour to change what we do with what we know. *English Journal, 107*(6), 26–30.

Colorado Department of Education (2020). *2020 Colorado academic standards in reading, writing, and communicating.* Retrieved from www.cde.state.co.us/standardsandinstruction/standards

Common Core State Standards Initiative (2010). *Common Core State Standards for English language arts.* Retrieved from www.corestandards.org

Duncan-Andrade, J., & Morrell, E. (2005). Turn up that radio, teacher: Popular cultural pedagogy in new century urban schools. *Journal of School Leadership, 15*(3), 284–304.

Fink, L.D. (2013). *Creating significant learning outcomes: An integrated approach to designing college courses.* San Francisco, CA: Jossey-Bass.

Fu, D. (2009). *Writing between languages: How English language learners make the transition to fluency, grades 4–12.* Portsmouth, NH: Heinemann.

Gay, G. (2002). Preparing for culturally responsive teaching. *Journal of Teacher Education, 53*(2), 106–116.

Grimes, N. (2002). *Bronx masquerade*. New York, NY: Dial Books.

Hmelo-Silver, C.E. (2004). Problem-based learning: What and how do students learn? *Educational Psychology Review, 16*, 235–266.

International Literacy Association (2017). *Literacy assessment: What everyone needs to know*. Literacy Leadership Brief. Retrieved from https://literacyworldwide.org/docs/default-source/where-we-stand/literacy-assessment-brief.pdf?sfvrsn=efd4a68e_4

International Literacy Association (2018). *Expanding the canon: How diverse literature can transform literacy learning*. Position Statement. Retrieved from https://www.literacyworldwide.org/docs/default-source/where-we-stand/ila-expanding-the-canon.pdf

International Literacy Association (2019). *Children's rights to read*. Retrieved May 24, 2019, from https://www.literacyworldwide.org/docs/default-source/resource-documents/ila-childrens-rights-to-read.pdf

Jacobs, H.H. (1997). *Mapping the big picture: Integrating curriculum & assessment K-12*. Alexandria, VA: ASCD.

Johnson, N.J., Koss, M.D., & Martinez, M. (2018). Through the sliding glass door: #Empowerthereader. *The Reading Teacher, 71*(5), 569–577.

Juliani, A.J. (2015). *Inquiry and innovation in the classroom: Using 20% time, genius hour, and PBL to drive student success*. New York, NY: Routledge.

Krebs, D., & Zvi, G. (2015). *The genius hour guidebook: Fostering passion, wonder, and inquiry in the classroom*. New York, NY: Routledge.

Lacy, A. (2019). Starting with students: A framework for high school reading. *English Journal, 108*(4), 17–20.

Ladson-Billings, G. (1995). Toward a theory of culturally relevant pedagogy. *American Educational Research Journal, 32*(3), 465–491.

Langer, J. (2011). *Envisioning literature: Literary understanding and literature instruction*. New York, NY: Teachers College.

Lee, V.S. (2012). What is inquiry-guided learning? *New Directions for Teaching and Learning, 129*, 5–14.

Lewison, M., Flint, A. S., & Van Sluys, K. (2002). Taking on critical literacy: The journey of newcomers and novices. *Language Arts, 79*(5), 382–392.

McConnell, C. (2011). *The essential questions handbook*. New York, NY: Scholastic.

McTighe, J., & Wiggins, G. (2013). *Essential questions: Opening doors to student understanding*. Alexandria, VA: ASCD.

National Council of Teachers of English (2018). *Literacy assessment: Definitions, principles, and practices*. Position Statement. Retrieved from https://ncte.org/statement/assessmentframingst/

National Council of Teachers of English (2019). *The NCTE position statement on independent reading*. Retrieved from https://ncte.org/statement/independent-reading/

National Councils of Teachers of English (2020). *Position paper on the role of English teachers in educating English language learners (ELLs)*. Position Paper. Retrieved from https://ncte.org/statement/teaching-english-ells/

Pearson, P.D., & Gallagher, M.C. (1983). The instruction of reading comprehension. *Contemporary Educational Psychology, 8,* 317–344.

Risko, V.J., & Walker-Dalhouse, D. (2012). *Be that teacher!: Breaking the cycle for struggling readers*. New York, NY: Teachers College.

Rosenblatt, L. (1968). *Literature as exploration*. New York, NY: Noble and Noble.

Virginia Department of Education (2017). *English standards of learning for Virginia public schools*. Retrieved from www.doe.virginia.gov/

WIDA (2012). *Amplification of the English language development standards: Kindergarten–Grade 12*. Retrieved from https://wida.wisc.edu/sites/default/files/resource/2012-ELD-Standards.pdf

Wiggins, G., & McTighe, J. (2005). *Understanding by design*. Upper Saddle River, NJ: Pearson.

Wiliam, D. (2013). Assessment: The bridge between teaching and learning. *Voices from the Middle, 21*(2), 15–20.

Wright, W.E. (2019). *Foundations for teaching English language learners: Research, theory, policy, and practice* (3rd ed.). Philadelphia, PA: Caslon.